Video in Social Science Research

In this digital age, the use of video in social science research has become commonplace. As the technological sophistication of video has increased along with usability, and as spiralling staff costs push out direct observation, the researchers training today are adopting video in ever greater numbers as they struggle to produce high quality research that is accessible. However, the 'fit' of video technology with research is far from simple.

Ideally placed to offer guidance to developing researchers, this new text draws together the theoretical, methodological and practical issues of effectively using video across the social sciences. This book concentrates on how researchers can benefit from the use of video in their own research, whether it is:

- video as representation;
- video as an aid to reflection;
- video that generates participation;
- video, voice and articulation; or
- video that acts as a provocation.

In turn, each of these five central functions is discussed in relation to different stages of the research process, consisting of:

- research design;
- fieldwork and data collection;
- analysis of data and findings; and
- dissemination.

As a practical research tool, this book shows how, why and when video should be used, representing an invaluable guide for postgraduate and doctoral students conducting research in the social sciences, as well as any researchers, academics or professionals interested in developing technologically informed research.

Kaye Haw is Principal Research Fellow in the School of Education at the University of Nottingham, UK.

Mark Hadfield is Professor of Education in the School of Education at the University of Wolverhampton, UK.

Video in Social Science Research

Functions and forms

Kaye Haw and
Mark Hadfield

Routledge
Taylor & Francis Group

LONDON AND NEW YORK

First edition published 2011
by Routledge
2 Park Square, Milton Park, Abingdon, Oxon, OX14 4RN

Simultaneously published in the USA and Canada
by Routledge
270 Madison Avenue, New York, NY 10016

Routledge is an imprint of the Taylor & Francis Group, an informa business

© 2011 Kaye Haw and Mark Hadfield

Typeset in Galliard by
Florence Production Ltd, Stoodleigh, Devon
Printed and bound in Great Britain by
TJ International Ltd, Padstow, Cornwall

British Library Cataloguing in Publication Data
A catalogue record for this book is available from the British Library

Library of Congress Cataloging-in-Publication Data
Haw, Kaye.
  Video in social science research: functions and forms /
Kaye Haw and Mark Hadfield.
      p. cm.
    1. Social sciences – Research – Audio-visual aids.   I. Hadfield,
Mark.   II. Title.
H62.2.H39 2011
300.72–dc22   2010019910

ISBN13: 978–0–415–46785–8 (hbk)
ISBN13: 978–0–415–46786–5 (pbk)
ISBN13: 978–0–203–83911–9 (ebk)

Contents

Figures

Tables

Introduction

This book differs from others in this area for three reasons. First, it makes a distinction between video as data, video production as a process for generating data, and the data-gathering potential of various video products at different stages in the research process. Second, to structure our exploration of video within social science research, we use a typology of five modalities that reflect the different contributions video makes to research from within different paradigms and traditions. Third, we introduce readers to key methodological constructs and issues that arise from the degree to which the video is integrated within and across differing stages of the research process, from recruitment to dissemination.

This is not a 'how to' book about making videos, although it does contain tasks for prospective video researchers, neither is it a theoretical discourse on the cultural significance of video, although we do explore the influence of cultural norms on the way in which video is used in research. This is a 'so what' book, in the sense that, drawing on our experiences of researching using video over the last twenty years, in a multiplicity of ways and across an eclectic mix of research projects, we set out to answer a number of 'so what' questions:

- So what do I need to think about before I consider using video in my research?
- So what are the potential benefits and issues associated with integrating video into different aspects of my research?

And, finally and most importantly, it asks critically:

- So what is all the fuss about?

For nearly twenty years, we have worked on a range of externally funded projects, many of them evaluations and applied pieces of research. During this time, we have by necessity had to draw on a number of paradigms and traditions, learning as we went along and adapting them to our own needs. Our approach to thinking about and working with video has therefore always been underpinned by a strong pragmatic sense, and this has influenced the structure of this book. The five modalities we use reflect this pragmatic perspective as they each represent specific uses video can be put to in various forms of research.

- Extraction: using video to record a specific interaction so that it can be studied in more depth by the researcher.
- Reflection: using video to support participants to reflect upon their actions, understandings and constructions.
- Projection and provocation: using video to provoke participants to critically examine and challenge existing norms, traditions and power structures.
- Participation: using video to engage participants in a research project in ways that allow them to shape its focus and outcomes.
- Articulation: using video to help participants voice their opinions and communicate these to others.

For us, these modalities occupy the mid-ground between broad research paradigms and methodologies and more specific research methods and tools. These modalities link together the work of numerous researchers and research projects in different research traditions across the social sciences. They do this because, within each modality, researchers are broadly using video for similar purposes, even if they disagree about what is meant by research and what its aims should be.

This book also sets out to critique some of the dominant discourses around the role of video. The current discourses tend to position video as either purely a data collection tool or a methodological novelty capable of serving almost any purpose, the Swiss Army knife of qualitative research. We believe these discourses dichotomise research traditions. It can lead to those interested in studying micro-interactions, who might spend hours analysing a few seconds of video, being dismissed as the 'nod and the wink club', with a limited understanding of the potentials and limitations of video. Contrastingly, those interested in video as a way of negotiating issues of empowerment, enablement and emancipation are constructed as a novelty act, the three 'Es' who lack an in-depth understanding of research and tend to conflate it with creative, political and therapeutic processes.

In this book, we not only want to challenge such crude caricatures but also explore the complex middle ground that exists between these extremes, but also to show how they are fundamentally linked by the purposes that lie behind their use of video. We also want to challenge the fashionability of working with video, based on the rather uncritical notion that its inclusion as a method or part of a methodology will somehow make the research more relevant. We want to make the reader 'pause for thought' and challenge the erroneous perception that using video is an easy option. Never confuse the ease of making a video with the very different process of using video in the research process. It is these issues that are highlighted from different perspectives in each of the chapters. Because Chapters 2–6 are each written around a different modality, they vary in style and structure. Each chapter, however, will be illustrated by reference to a range of different projects and methodologies to allow readers to consider the extent to which they want to integrate video into their research and the purposes they wish it to serve. Although the chapters are all different, both in style and length, they all begin with a root metaphor to encapsulate and draw out the potential and limitations of video in a particular modality. These are our metaphors, and we use them because we actively use metaphorical thinking within our research designs. We believe that, if we want to see video being used more effectively and creatively, we need to develop better metaphors that describe its potential.

The book can be read in many different ways. Chapters 7 and 8 are doing, designing and planning chapters and could be read first. It would also be a good idea to look at the relevant parts of Chapters 7 and 8 after reading a specific chapter. The book is both theoretically and practically driven, and therefore we use the first chapter to give a broad overview of our approach, explain why we think this is an appropriate way to look at the role of video in research and chart our own experiences. Each chapter is written to stand alone, but the chapters obviously overlap, and for this reason we would strongly advise that Chapters 3 and 4, on reflection, and projection and provocation, be read together, and similarly, Chapters 5 and 6, on participation and articulation. We end this introduction with a brief descriptor of the chapters.

Chapter 1: Forms and functions

This chapter provides a brief introduction to the use of video with reference to five key modalities: extraction, reflection, projection, participation and voice. These modalities describe how video has been used to generate deeper insights into different issues in the pursuit of various forms of knowledge, praxis and change. It is in two sections. The first provides a brief overview of the way in which the use of video has developed in the social sciences. The second positions our own work with respect to these modalities by highlighting some of our own video projects, using a narrative trajectory to explore lessons learnt.

Chapter 2: Video used in extractive mode

Possibly the most widespread use of video has been as a means of capturing a representation of the phenomenon under study. These representations can range from those created by researchers themselves, often replacing direct observation when it was too costly, dangerous or intrusive, to those video artefacts created by an individual or subculture under study. Based around examples of research into teaching and learning within classrooms, this chapter provides an introduction to the key theoretical and practical issues of using video. The focus is on whether using video in this way presents different data collection and analytical challenges.

Chapter 3: Using video in a reflective mode

From the earliest incarnation of video, its playback facility has led to it being used as a means of prompting reflection by both the participants and audiences of research. This chapter considers how video can be used to prompt differing forms of reflection using the metaphor of the mirror and ideas of pause and translation. It gives an introduction to the key theoretical and practical issues that researchers need to consider, and explores the role of video as both a stimulus and a means of recording participants' reflections within different theories of reflection. It also looks at the differences between individual and group prompts.

Chapter 4: Video as projection and provocation

Using video as a form of provocation is an extension to its use as a stimulus for reflection. This chapter looks at how video as provocation sets out to create 'argumentative' and occasionally confrontational processes and products, based on exploring tensions, dilemmas and contradictions within a given social context or process. This 'critical' approach can have a number of purposes, from the 'emancipation' of individuals from a particular ideological perspective, through challenging stereotypical beliefs to breaking down routinised behaviour. To achieve this critical approach, the video process needs to support the participants and the audiences of research to consider and acknowledge their own positioning, their value positions, and prompt them to change.

Chapter 5: Video that generates participation

The aims of participatory research vary from social action researchers who see it as a means of developing civic involvement, and particularly as a way of including marginalised groups, to critical ethnographers whose commitment to an 'insider' perspective requires that research be carried out at least in part by members of a given community. This chapter looks at the issues that arise when working in this way by highlighting two of our projects, Urbanfields and 'Seen but not heard', to consider how video can be used to facilitate access and negotiate a focus for the work, and its potential and limitations when managing relationships.

Chapter 6: Video, voice and articulation

The notion that video can support those who are often silenced or excluded breaks it out of the confines of traditional academic research into the arena of researchers who are interested in supporting others to develop and articulate their own voices and achieve broader social changes. This chapter explores different conceptions of 'voice' and the role video can play in articulating them. It examines how video production interacts with key methodological issues, such as the extent to which participants maintain control, the power relationships between researchers and participants, and how to influence target audiences.

Chapter 7: Video and your research: function and forms

Chapter 7 is based around a series of research 'design' tasks, two for each modality, that allows the reader to explore how to relate the technical and aesthetic aspects of video to the theoretical and analytical dimensions of a research project. It aims to give those researchers who are 'video novices' an insight into the practical and technical demands, and limitations, of different approaches. By the end of this chapter, readers will have identified the particular functions they wish video to serve in their research projects and the most appropriate form for it to take.

Chapter 8: Video and your research: from methodology to methods

This chapter is based around a number of planning tools that will guide the reader through the process of integrating video into different stages of the research process. The chapter is non-technical, taking the reader through four broad research stages – recruitment, entry and access, data generation, and data analysis and dissemination. The chapter contains a consideration of the specific ethical issues raised by the use of video in social science research. Each section of this chapter finishes with a set of practical dos and don'ts.

Video raises a number of questions and problems that may not necessarily arise using more traditional methods and materials in the social sciences. We hope this book demystifies some of them, but, on the whole, for us the challenge of working with video is its immediacy, its vibrancy, which allows us to work more collectively and critically and its ability to bring a range of people into the research process in ways that they perhaps would never have considered possible.

Chapter 1

Forms and functions

In an age in which visual imagery is challenging the authority of written text in a range of domains, from youth culture to news reporting (Featherstone, 1995; McRobbie, 2000), it has become a type of 'nexus', a connection point between researchers that straddles methodologies and disciplines, from the academic to the applied. At this nexus, debates between researchers over visual methodologies tend to fall into a number of distinct camps. Dominant among these are those with a long tradition in visual methods and the use of visual materials, for example ethnographers and anthropologists (MacCannell, 1994; Banks, 1995; Margolis, 1998), and those methodologies where an extensive technology for observing research subjects has developed, for example classroom-based research within education (Noyes, 2004, 2008). These camps are the basis of the traditional distinction between visual research that focuses on 'subjects' consumption and appreciation, or 'participants' production, of visual forms and research where visual methodologies are controlled by researchers as they study a particular phenomenon. This is a distinction based on who consumes, owns and produces visual images, whose purposes they serve and to whom they have a specific meaning, a distinction summarised by Banks (2007) as 'on the one hand between the use of images to study society and, on the other, the sociological study of images' (p. 7).

There is a wide range of visual methodologies, from virtual/visual ethnography to participatory video research, and methods range from mind mapping to 'phototherapy'. At times, the only apparent connection seems to be the interest of researchers in visual representations and individuals', or their own, understanding of the 'reality' that surrounds them. Implicit in most discussions, and explicit in a few, is a concern with the nature of the connection between seeing and knowing. For naïve and radical empiricists alike, seeing truly is 'believing', and the status given to the visual data can lead researchers to adopt various forms of visualism, 'the view that, among our phenomenal experiences, only visual experiences are evidence' (Bealer, 1999, p. 248). However, there are others who stress the materiality of the visual form and the contexts, both symbolic and physical, within which it is produced or consumed. Form and context can not only constrain what can be depicted or captured visually, but also give additional meaning to visual products, which act as a 'representation of a representation' (Banks, 2001, p. 50). From within this perspective, what is of primary interest is the symbolic meaning of a video or picture created within a social relationship, whereas the 'literal reality' captured by its content is only of secondary interest.

In this book, we focus upon one particular stratum of visual methodologies – the mechanical production of moving images or, more specifically, video. Our reasons for focusing on video are threefold.

First, as researchers, we have grown up with the technology, from bulky VHS cameras that had to rest on your shoulder to the new HD digital cameras, no bigger than a mobile phone. Our own use of video has developed over the last fifteen years, from it simply being an additional form of data collection to using it to create critical dialogue between groups involved in community consultations and, more recently, as a means of exploring group self-representation and collective and individual identity.

Second, the sheer fashionability of video, both within and outside the research community, has made it one of the most popular visual method- ologies. Video is now as likely to be used by researchers who are interested in it, not for internal, methodological reasons, but for what might be called 'external' reasons, to do with its cultural cachet, perceived persuasive power and potential to democratise the research process. Hence its popularity within participatory, emancipatory and social action forms of research, where it is treated as a medium with the capacity to engage a mass or non-specialist audiences with the processes and outcomes of research (Braden, 1999).

Third, video occupies a very paradoxical position within the visual nexus. At one level, its ability to capture moving images with a high degree of naturalism, and to allow for these images to be examined with far greater intensity than would be possible by direct observation, gives it an aura of hyperrealism. Video has the potential to capture behaviours and interactions in situations where direct human observation would be too intrusive, and in ways and forms, from slow motion to multiple perspectives, that provide additional and novel forms of data. At another level, we live in an era in which the media, the third culture (Featherstone, 1995), are dominated by video formats, from the 2 GB uploads of the so-called YouTube generation to the

Hollywood blockbusters that can be watched via our mobile phones and game consoles. Video is therefore strongly encamped in differing parts of the nexus. In those with a strong visual methods tradition, it often becomes entangled with much broader theoretical debates around visual forms of knowing and representation, whereas, in others, it is ensnared in the specific technical challenges of collecting and analysing observational data. Video has even spawned its own partial methodological solution to this paradoxical status, in the work of participative and collaborative projects in which participants and researchers review and analyse existing video materials, as well as produce new materials.

Video is well established within key aspects of a range of different research processes. Possibly the most widespread use of video has been as a form of 'indirect' observation, allowing for detailed coding of individual and group behaviours, and as a means of prompting reflection by participants on their decision-making and actions. In applied and evaluative research, it has found favour as a way of assessing the fidelity of implementation of new interventions. As a form of disseminating research findings, especially for practitioners, it has now become ubiquitous in many disciplines. Recent developments within new digital technologies have created new means of video-based interaction and dissemination, from web-based distribution to video-conferencing. This, in combination with the wider availability of commercial-quality equipment and software, has allowed researchers to work differently together in teams, with participants and prospective users of their research, and to create new forms of virtual networks and spaces for enhanced analysis, dialogue and dissemination. The use of video has grown in popularity, not only because of the increased availability of new technology and the relative increase in cost of direct observation, but also because of the cultural cachet associated with it as a medium.

The very plasticity of video as a research tool and its presence across fragmented fields of research means that individuals have different concerns at the forefront of their minds when they discuss its use. This diversity was apparent in the findings of our current Economic and Social Research Council (ESRC) project aimed at promoting critical dialogue concerning the methodological issues arising from working with young people, voice and video within participatory research. Their concerns could be grouped into three broad categories: first, integrating theoretical strands concerned with video and participation; second, the issue of developing a theoretical and contextual background for video analysis; and third, issues to do with the notion of voice. We too have long held concerns about the problematic notion of voice in relation to the type of voice being articulated, who and what is heard, what is listened to and how it is heard (see Hadfield and Haw, 2000b, 2001; Haw, 2006c). It is these concerns about the types and power of different voices that have positioned the developing body of our work in relation to video and young people.

As it stands, we believe that researchers in this area, in common with others, are having predominantly two types of conversation, the ones about the technical and creative aspects of using video in research, and those that are about their own positioning within the research. However, our research is directed by the belief that there is a third level of conversation to be had, and this is one that focuses on the degree of integration of video within the research process, which, when combined with questions about the type of research being undertaken, becomes linked to the relationships between the researchers and participants. Our contention is that the dialogue around the first two conversations is existent and rich, if bounded by particular disciplines, but the critical dialogue between these and the third conversation is under-developed and under-theorised.

The purpose of this book is to alert expert and novice researchers using video to the importance of being part of this critical dialogue, and our contribution is to come at it from a perspective based on our particular interpretation of the concept of modes and modalities. The concept of multimodality is borrowed from linguistics (see Iedema, 2003; Kress and Van Leeuwen, 2001). Linguists are careful to make the distinction between modes and media. Modes are:

> The abstract, non-material resources of meaning making (obvious ones include writing, speech and images; less obvious ones include gesture, facial expression, texture, size and shape, even colour). Media, on the other hand, are the specific material forms in which modes are realized, including tools and materials.
>
> (Dicks *et al.*, 2006, referencing Kress and Van Leeuwen, 2001, p. 22)

We take the view that modes are abstract meaning-making resources, and so, for our purposes, modalities are the abstract purposes for which video is used, rather than video as a medium, process, tool or product. Others have also found the concept of multimodality useful when discussing visual methodologies. Rose, for example, suggests that there are three modalities that can contribute to a critical understanding of visual images, the technological, compositional and social (Rose, 2008). Our point here is that the concept of modality is used in different ways, reflecting the particular background and discipline of the users, and that we, in our approach to exploring the forms and functions of video, are using it in our own pragmatic way.

Positioning our own work

The rise of the media society in which young people draw on 'third cultures' (Featherstone, 1995), mass-medial cultures, as part of their social construction of identity has been well documented (see McRobbie, 2000) as a social and cultural phenomenon within youth culture. The increased use of video across the social sciences is well documented (Prosser, 1992, 1998; Banks, 1995, 2001; Niesyto *et al.*, 2001; Pink, 2001; Voithofer, 2005; Rose, 2008). It is also considered to be a powerful dissemination medium for a range of projects concerned with young people. For these reasons, there has been a massive expansion in the use of video with young people by a range of professionals and campaign organisations trying to ensure that their voice is heard within local decision-making. The National Youth Agency and British Film Institute (Harvey *et al.*, 2005) estimated in 2005 that there were 17,000 young people being given video training, with thousands more involved in video projects with no training. Video production has become a popular approach, as it is seen as a means of increasing the participation of young people within civic life and education, particularly those deemed alienated or disaffected (Johnson, 2001; Tolman *et al.*, 2001; Kincade and Macy, 2003). The overlapping of global cultures with specific local and social cultures has been discussed by researchers involved in media or critical literacy studies (see Niesyto *et al.*, 2001); their findings, however, have been difficult for non-specialist researchers to apply systematically to their own research.

Young people are frequently used as an example of how individuals have become increasingly sophisticated in their media consumption and the increasing role it plays in their self-construction, and this affects their reaction to video within research. For example, within participatory projects, researchers need to provide a complex mix of technical, creative and critical support to move people from consumers to producers of media. The impact of these forms of support and how they interact with the experiences of participants as media consumers sets up methodological issues that range from questions of ownership to the authenticity of any video products.

Our own work with video has been developed over previous research projects working with marginalised groups and communities on a range of sensitive issues. These studies have ranged from issues around racism, through issues of exclusion from school and perceptions of full-body search procedures in prisons, to the most recent participatory research. In each research project, video was used slightly differently, depending on the objectives of the research and the types of participants or audiences it aimed to engage in the work, but each of these pieces of research had a common aim (see Hadfield and Haw, 1997b, 2001, 2003; Haw *et al.*, 1999; Haw, 2002, 2006b): that was, to legitimate a range of voices through creating a series of spaces for critical dialogue and action. We have used video as a professional development and community consultation tool, and as a means to explore group self-representation, and collective and individual identity (Melucci 1989, 1996). This way of working with video is not unique within the UK context (see Gauntlett, 2007, and the associated website: www.theory.org.uk). What we do have is a broad range of experience in using video in a great many pieces of research. We briefly describe the following projects because each presented different methodological challenges and we refer back to them throughout the book to highlight how we have learnt to deal with them.

IPSUP

Our first extensive use of video was on a European funded project, IPSUP, an acronym for International Projects on Schools and Urban Policy. It was in this project that we first came across the work of Dirk Schouten and his ideas about emancipatory action research linked to professional development activities. We acted as second-order action researchers (Elliott, 1991), supporting the work of a group of practitioners. These practitioners were enrolled in a Masters programme that looked at the development and implementation of public policies within urban contexts. It was run jointly between a university in England and another in the Netherlands. The programme had a strong comparative element, based around joint visits and a number of satellite link-ups. During these link-ups, a series of video case studies, created by the course participants in both universities, were used to look at how, in different countries and cities, policy issues were constructed and services developed responses to them. The MA programme was designed to attract senior managers and leaders from a range of services, both public and voluntary. The cohorts of students in each university were supported by small teams of researchers and video consultants who assisted them in making their video case studies. The videos produced as part of the IPSUP project ranged along the continuum, from relatively straightforward accounts of a policy issue, to highly personal, reflective accounts of the response of an individual to a new policy discourse. From this, we learned a great deal about the potential of the video production process to prompt reflection and to generate data.

Single Regeneration Budget (SRB) evaluation

Our next study using video was an evaluation aiming to assess the impact of a massive amount of European funding to regenerate four socio-economically deprived areas of Nottingham. The objective of this evaluation was to match the concerns of policy developers with those of local people and maintain the engagement of local people throughout the process. To do this, the team adopted a way of working with video that we described as '*real-time*' *ethnography*. The research was carried out within the same time span of the local policy development cycle or life span of the funding framework from which most post-16 educational provision was funded. This gave the process its 'real-time' element, in that the spaces created for voices to be heard were timed so that they could influence the political and policy processes. The evaluation used a mixture of focus groups, video case studies, local media, formal reports and large-scale household surveys as a means of juxtaposing different voices. Aspects of the large-scale survey were combined with 'vox pops' from local people to create an initial stimulus for a series of focus groups of local residents. These focus groups were recorded and edited into the original tape to create a stimulus for a series of focus groups with professionals; this was our first use of a 'trigger tape'. These focus groups were in turn recorded, and extracts were added to the original 'trigger tape', and this was then presented to a focus group of funders and senior managers. Finally, all the materials were developed into a final dissemination tape. This piece of work marked the start of our thinking about how to combine non-threatening contexts in which people were able to voice their views with video materials that prompted critical reflection, video as a 'projective device'. Our interest was in the potential of a video stimulus to prompt individuals to engage in, and 'challenge', the issues it raised. We wanted participants to project their views and beliefs onto the stimulus as we saw this as being less threatening than having to critically engage with issues raised by other individuals within the group. During this project, we undertook our first group analysis of video involving researchers and those present within the focus groups. The power of group analysis is its potential to generate multiple interpretations of singular events and its usefulness in helping us refine the 'critical power' of the video stimulus materials led us to develop this approach in future projects. We also realised that group analysis of video involving researchers and participants required both good facilitation and sophisticated recording techniques.

'Seen but not heard'

Our video learning curve was also influenced by a project we called the 'Seen but not heard' project. For this research, we worked with a group of young people who had been excluded from a particular school. This is one of our pieces of work that we discuss more fully in later chapters, where we look at the role of video in generating participation and articulating voice. In the project, we worked with the young people as co-researchers within a team that included us as university researchers, their teachers and their youth workers, to make a video targeted at the school management to tell them what it felt like to be excluded from their school. Their completed video was a mixture of interviews and role play presented in a news-based format. On the basis of this research, we realised the need for a conceptual framework for differentiating the forms of voice that were being developed through different types of participation within the team and their link with certain research methods and agendas. Methodologically, we also became very aware of the issues to do with the integration of a research project within a broader change process and, specifically, the management of a range of stakeholders when dealing with critical video-texts.

Perceptions and experiences of full body searching

The following project features in the chapter on projection and provocation because, in it, we developed our thinking from how to use video as a reflective tool to how we could use it to help its audience be critically reflective with us. To research the experiences and perceptions of prisoners and prison officers with regard to full body searching, we used a range of research tools. The very different contexts in which strip-searching occurs, the various purposes it serves and the impact this has on the perceptions of those involved meant that we had to devise materials that drew out the process and sequencing of strip-searching. We produced two separate short videos based around a re-enactment of a male and female fully body, or strip, search where the soundtrack was predominantly interviews with prisoners and prison workers. These videos were conceived to have a range of purposes. First, they helped sequence the whole full body search process, allowing for it to be broken down so that it could then be reconstructed during individual and group discussions. Second, they helped the participants to take the research more seriously, because the videos used the voices and opinions of their peers, thus challenging cultural norms of silence on this issue. This also allowed them to reflect upon issues more critically and helped them to articulate feelings and insights by focusing on key aspects of the search process that were deemed problematic or controversial. Third, the video helped them reflect and articulate points they wished to make about how to make the process more effective and less demeaning. Last, the video helped negotiate access and recruitment by showing video materials that conveyed the meaning of the research and established its importance and integrity through conveying initial ideas about how to make the process more effective. The individual and group discussions engendered by the video stimulus material served to inform the development of a more meaningful and valid questionnaire that was used across six prisons.

Urbanfields

As we developed our usage of video in these different modalities, we also became more sophisticated in how it could be integrated more fully in the research process. Increasingly we were doing research that was engaging with hard-to-reach or marginalised groups on sensitive areas of their everyday lives. Urbanfields set out to provide a detailed description of the direct experiences of 'risk', as detailed by black and Asian young people themselves. To date, it is one of the most complex pieces of research we have undertaken. The research explored the ways in which being a member of a minority community both protected and exposed young people to risk. The build-up of individual representations of everyday life was done through young people making their own videos about their lives, the use of a series of trigger videos, and us as researchers making a final video product using a compilation of these materials to be used with a range of professionals working with young people. This was a complex project in which video was both fully integrated and multimodal. Our issues concerned how to incorporate materials produced by young people, community researchers and professional video makers into a cohesive product aimed at a wide range of professionals working with young people. This involved the use of audio and video extracts, titling and the 'flagging up' of a range of contentious areas using questions put in the form of equations to stimulate discussion. The project also made extensive use of community-based researchers who supported the core research team. They were recruited because of the nature of the local community and the difficulty in engaging young people within research that is looking at involvement in crime. These community-based researchers were working in potentially dangerous situations on sensitive subjects, within a community in which they were known. This required the development of a number of protocols to support them and ensure their safety.

From hijab to jilbab

In the last project we highlight in this book, one of our most recent ones, members of a particular Muslim community were invited to participate in making a video that was in part conceived of as an act of resistance to how they are being stereotypically positioned by others. The purpose of the research was to study the shifting identities of British Muslims by returning to the same participants and their families who had taken part in a piece of doctoral research carried out over a decade ago. The research explored how the women who had taken part in the original research while still school-children had since constructed their identities now they were adults, many with their own children and in employment. The aim was to produce a film that provoked those outside Muslim communities to rethink how they viewed Muslims, while at the same time reflecting on how they themselves are being positioned within their own social norms and discourses, often through the media, which encourage them to view these communities in a particular way. The video produced at the end of this project was aimed at audiences of young people in formal and informal education settings, to promote discussions around issues of identities, Britishness and citizenship. In its conception, it had many similarities to our other video products, but we were making a DVD, not at the beginning of a project to broach a strong taboo such as full body searching, but at the end of a project. Our aim here was to produce a film that, by representing findings not obviously in the public psyche, could stimulate a process of re-attunement and therefore a more reflexive dialogue.

Video and voice

Given this trajectory, it is perhaps unsurprising that our last and most recent project funded by the ESRC is a methodological one designed to explore the issues that arise from working with the voice of young people in participatory projects using video. In the first phase, we designed an online questionnaire. This survey aimed to gain responses from approximately 100 projects about the methodological and ethical issues they had faced. To support reflection, each questionnaire was accompanied by a 'trigger' DVD, showing a selection of video-based scenarios illustrating key issues, which we created from our own research working with young people and video and put together as a series of short video clips. From our analysis of the responses, we identified six projects as case studies. The aim of these case studies was not to produce a series of accounts of what people had been involved in, but to look at some of the key methodological issues they had faced. Once we had collected their accounts, we created short video clips of their projects and their discussions of the work. The case studies were chosen to represent people with different backgrounds, from academics to community workers to professional organisations, and a range of experience with using video, from the novice to the more experienced. We put these case studies, together with ours, onto a final DVD and built an accompanying website. You can access this at www.videoandvoice.co.uk.

On the basis of the existing literature, we created an initial model of the key factors that, in combination, would position how researchers would construct the main methodological and ethical issues within participatory video. We described this model as a 'nexus' as it consisted of an intersection of three theoretical themes within the literature:

1   the overall aim behind adopting a participatory approach;
2   the nature and the degree of participation by young people;
3   the degree to which video was integrated within the research process.

Our initial theoretical assumption was that the construction of both methodological and ethical issues by the respondents would arise from the juxtaposition of the forms of participatory research they were involved in, their view on, and usage of, 'video' and their relationships with the young people they were working with. The literature review revealed that there were relatively few detailed accounts of research that encompassed all three themes, but numerous ones that covered two out of three, or were partial descriptions. The review still left unanswered questions about methodological and ethical issue such as:

• Were there distinct issues that arose specifically because of the interactions of video, participatory research and young people?
• Were there issues of such significance in any of these three themes that they defined/dominated the nature of their interactions?

- Which issues, or interactions, have most affected the form of projects being undertaken and presented the greatest challenges to researchers?

Our main finding was that the initial model, which drew heavily from existing participatory research literature, did not sufficiently recognise the impact that video as a process, as well as a product, had on shaping the methodological and ethical issues faced by researchers. This finding emerged from differences between the questionnaire responses from novice and more-experienced participatory video researchers and within the case studies and seminars. It suggests that there is a series of largely unrecognised methodological and ethical issues that novice 'video' researchers, their supervisors, ethics committees and funders need to be made aware of. This is not to say that widely recognised issues concerned, within participatory research, around power relationships between researchers and young people and the ownership of the research process were not widely discussed. In fact, they dominated many of the conversations of less-experienced 'video' researchers. Key issues among these conversations were:

1   The nature of the partnership between researchers and young people. Specifically, to what extent researchers and professionals support them in the creative and technical aspects of video production processes and the extent to which this affects the authenticity and criticality of the voice of young people.
2   The extent to which researchers developed young people's understanding of the audiences of the research and were involved in the presentations of their materials to others.
3   The gap between the experiences of young people as video consumers and the need to critically engage with the expectations these create and their ability to be video producers of materials that articulated their perspectives and have the potential to effect change.

More experienced researchers did not claim to have resolved such issues; rather, they tended to recognise they could only be ameliorated and were highly affected by the demands of funders and the limitations of resources. They discussed a differing order of issues, key among which were:

1   An acute awareness of the differing ethical issues associated with the integration of video into differing stages of the research process, from the collection of data, or filming, to the dissemination of findings, the ethics of broadcasting or programming.
2   A deeper understanding of the possibilities and limitations of differing treatments of the video production process; these ranged from seeing

it as a 'structuring device', within which participants were actively encouraged to reflect upon their views and were supported in consciously articulating them, to others who treated it more as a 'mediated space' in which the process of production provided a context in which young people were more likely to reveal their perceptions and views, when compared with more traditional data collection processes, such as interviews.

3   A greater ability to manage the interconnections between the function of video products, both within the research process, often as reflective tools, and as research outputs, where they might be concerned with influencing others, with the overall quality and nature of young people's participation within the research and video process; more experienced researchers not only showed more sophistication in their use of video products, but also greater awareness of the likely responses of potential audiences to differing forms of these products; this awareness affected the design of both the research processes and video production.

A key concern shared by all researchers was the impact of the general social discourse around the use of video with young people, which was marked by high levels of concern and suspicion. Again, researchers differed in their responses, with more-experienced researchers feeling more able to challenge often ill-founded concerns over 'identification' of participants; they had a stronger recognition of young people's own agency with regard to their digital identities, and the impact this had upon issues of ownership and usage of digital materials, and were more aware of the possibilities and limitations of alternative means of representation, such as dramatic reconstructions and the use of dramaturgical approaches. We have included such an extensive review of this project because its findings have heavily influenced our thinking about what areas this book needed to cover.

Summary of key projects (all materials are available from www.videoandvoice.co.uk)

In the following chapters, we unpick many of the methodological lessons we have been taught by working with video in different modalities. We draw on the projects we have highlighted here, refer to others we have worked on, where relevant, and the work of others to highlight specific methodological and ethical issues that seem to coalesce around video as a research tool. The aim is to both soothe and calm but also to give pause for thought to those researchers thinking of using video in their work.

Table 1.1 Summary of key projects

Date	Name of project	Available materials
1995–7	IPSUP: This two-year project involved professionals in England and the Netherlands producing video-based case studies of key urban policy issues. These cases formed the basis of a series of satellite link-ups and visits as they explored the ways in which they had constructed and responded to them.	None available
1997–9	SRB evaluation: This three-year study assessed the impact of SRB and URBAN funding in four areas of Nottingham. We worked with local communities to produce video materials, to act as trigger material for focus group interviews with residents, professionals and funders in each area. These videos formed the central part of a 'bottom-up' community assessment of SRB and URBAN funding.	Booklet *Community consultation* (hard copy)
1997–8	Family viewing: This project produced three video case studies of how different groups of young people from a range of ethnic minority communities combat, with the help of their communities and families, the impact of racism and xenophobia. In the UK, the project worked with long-established Asian and African-Caribbean communities in the East Midlands where there is a high level of unemployment.	DVD *Family viewing*
1998–9	'Seen but not heard': This participatory project worked with a group of young men on issues around exclusion from school. It addressed the aim of the funders to ensure that preventive and family support work takes note of the 'voice of the child' – in this case through 'social-action' participative research.	Booklet *Seen but not heard*
2002–3	Perceptions and experiences of full body searching: The research used a range of research tools to find out about attitudes of prisoners and their families to full body search procedures. We created two separate short videos for prisoners and prison officers based on a series of qualitative interviews with prisoners and prison workers and existing training and induction materials for staff and prisoners.	DVD Trigger tape used in project

Table 1.1 continued

Date	Name of project	Available materials
2001–5	Urbanfields: This project set out to provide a detailed description of the direct experiences of 'risk' as detailed by black and Asian young people themselves. We wanted to explore the ways in which being a member of a minority community both protects as well as exposes young people to risk.	DVD *Urbanfields*, plus academic articles
2007–9	From hijab to jilbab: An inter-generational piece of research that aimed to show shifts and changes within a particular Muslim community and everyday lives through interviews and video diaries.	DVD *Being and becoming*, plus academic articles
2007–10	Video and voice: A national review of participatory research projects that set out to use video and involve the voice of young people. Its aim was to produce materials that set out the key methodological and ethical issues facing these projects and how they can be addressed in practice.	DVD and website www. videoand voice.co.uk

Chapter 2

Video used in extractive mode

The use of video, and its predecessor film, as a means of capturing social phenomena so that they can be analysed in more detail later on has a lengthy history, and its popularity means that there are few forms of research into social interactions that have not explored its potential. As such, the arguments that surround video being used in this way reflect many of the broad, historical methodological debates that shape the social sciences. It therefore provides a good way of introducing both novice and expert researchers to a number of the key theoretical and practical issues they need to consider as they set out to use video within their research.

In this particular modality, 'raw' video footage is constructed as data, the video camera as a data collection tool, and the edited and analysed video as a means of illustrating and communicating any findings. In keeping with these constructions of video and its associated technologies, we have structured the chapter around four interconnected questions:

- What kind of data is video?
- What shapes the kinds of video material we extract from any situation?
- Does video require a different approach to analysis?
- What are the key issues when using video to show your findings?

Your answers to these questions should shape the design of your research and the way in which you integrate video into your research project. To help answer them we refer to our own work that has fallen within this modality. This has been mainly based in the area of what Hall (2000) describes as 'classroom videography', the use of video to study the interactions and learning of pupils and teachers. The applied use of film and video to understand and improve professional practices has a lengthy history and had its origins in the sort of multidisciplinary research that saw anthropologists,

linguists and psychiatrists studying family interaction during therapy sessions (Bateson *et al.*, 1971). Classroom videography is a good area in which to explore the possibilities and problems of the extractive use of video, because of the complexity of classrooms and the range and subtlety of the social interactions they contain. It also represents one of the most mature areas of study, because of the early adoption of video within education, not only to help improve the practice of those involved, but also to use these materials as part of wider professional development and knowledge transfer activities. The lengthy history of projects within this area that have not resulted in substantive and systemic improvements is a good basis for developing a critical understanding of the potential of video in applied research.

The root metaphor

It is perhaps no surprise that our preferred root metaphor for thinking about how video is used in this modality is that of the instant replay format used within sports broadcasting. Instant replays are used to examine significant moments within an overall event in greater detail. They extract from a game a key passage of play, a controversial decision by a match official or an exceptional piece of skill and make it available for comment by presenters and analysts. Replay technology provides analysts and commentators with additional information and the ability to manipulate the video record. They can examine an event from multiple perspectives, more than would have been available to any one participant or observer during an actual game, and these can be reviewed in slow motion. A part of the replay can be 'toggled', so that a specific point in time, such as the moment a ball hits a line on the ground, can be moved forward and backward in time to allow for the ball's trajectory and where it hit to be checked and rechecked. A particular part of the picture can be highlighted and magnified, so that what might have been seen initially as a trivial part of the sequence is now foregrounded. In some sports, additional data are added to supplement the video sequence; for example, a slowed-down spectrograph of the audio accompanies the replay so that any spikes in the graph, indicating an increase in noise, can be related to the video sequence and therefore help the sports analyst make judgements about if a ball hit the bat. Some sports have even used thermal imaging cameras to highlight 'hotspots' caused by the friction of a ball. During a replay, the sports analysts may also bring in footage from earlier on in the game, or even from different games, to allow for comparisons to be made between similar incidents or how individual players act, or to assess the consistency of match officials' decisions. With all this technical sophistication, the interpretation of replays can still be ambiguous: even with slow motion and multiple perspectives, analysts may still be uncertain about 'what really happened' and have to bow to the authority of the match officials who were actually 'there'. Finally, although those involved in the incident that is the focus of the replay are occasionally asked to give their view of what happened, they are not generally given access to the detailed replay or the analysts' comments, and their views are treated as just another source of evidence to add to that which has already been collected.

The 'sports replay' is a powerful root metaphor for thinking about the extractive use of video in social science research as it highlights a number of key characteristics:

- Video is seen as having captured a detailed representation of an observable phenomenon, which can then be removed from its context for further study.
- Video makes this phenomenon open to more detailed analysis than direct observation, as it allows for repeated showings, can be slowed

down, can be combined with other data sources and allows for multiple researchers to consider the same phenomenon.

- Video allows for the analysis of a social phenomenon at increasingly finer levels of granularity, moving from whole events to microseconds, and from broad patterns of social interaction to the nuances of facial expressions.
- The main purpose of this analysis is to inform the understanding of the researcher, the sports commentator or analyst, rather than the participants, the player.

What kind of data is video?

Probably the most common adjective applied to video as a form of data is that it is 'rich' data; running a close second would be 'multilayered'. These descriptions are based on comparing video with other forms of data commonly used within the social sciences. For example, it is rich in comparison with a recording of an interview, as it not only contains audio data but also captures visual data of nonverbal interactions. Similarly, it contains more information than could be captured by even the most detailed observation sheet.

Somewhat paradoxically, on other occasions, video comes off less well when compared with other forms of data collection approach. It can be treated as inferior to direct observation by a researcher. For example, as a means of generating understanding of complex social interaction, the camera can provide only a limited field of vision and struggles to convey all of the nuances and emotions that give specific meaning to an interaction. This apparently contradictory status that video has, through being constructed as both rich and partial, arises from two broad sets of issues. The first is to do with whether we treat video as a form of data or as a form of information from which data can be generated. The second is to do with the extent we see it as an objective record, or at least a source that can be 'objectified', or as being highly influenced by technical limitations and the subjectivity of researchers.

The starting point to unpacking these issues is to take a step back and ask ourselves the question 'What can a single piece of video give us data about?' Here, the multilayered nature of video comes into play, as a single piece of video has the potential to provide data about a range of differing foci, the four main ones being:

(a) the specific social interactions captured on it;

(b) participants' understanding of these interactions;

(c) the interpretations of those involved in creating the video;

(d) the frameworks through which individuals view the video.

When employed in an extractive modality, video is normally used to provide data about (a) and (b). In later chapters, we discuss why, in a participative modality, (c) becomes much more of a focus. This is because what people choose to film and how they film it can become almost as important a source of data as the content of what they actually record. Similarly, when employed within a reflective modality, one of the key uses of video is to help capture individual interpretations and constructions of the video being watched, or the things that it prompts viewers to reflect on, and so here (d) is the type of data being sought. Unfortunately, criticisms of the use of video often range across differing foci and then conflate them. In dealing with any methodological and theoretical criticisms, researchers therefore need to understand the focus they actually apply to. This book covers each of these foci as it covers the varying modalities within which video is used.

Within this particular modality, probably the most commonly cited criticism of video is that it is used to make assertions about the intentions and perspectives of participants (b), when it actually only contains data about 'visible' behaviours (a) (Wagner, 2006). This argument takes us back to the first of our two key issues, that is, the degree to which video is treated as primary data, or is more a source of information from which data can be generated, and so is seen as 'secondary' data. The decision as to whether any source of data is treated as primary or secondary is based upon the directness of the connection between it and the focus of the research. Most researchers are familiar with treating audio recordings of interviews as primary data, if they are interested in capturing the views or interpretation of a subject about an event, and then supplementing this with 'secondary' data, such as documentary records of the event. In these situations, any secondary data need to be connected with other sources of data to be generative of further insights or deeper understanding than that provided by the interview. Video, in this instance, is no different to other forms of data, and its status will therefore depend upon the extent to which the phenomena under study are visible or have to be operationalised to make them available to be captured on video. When using video, operationalising a phenomenon or construct means creating a clear association between it and a particular set of behaviours or actions captured on video. To an extent, this is the same with all forms of observational data, in that any researcher ticking an observation sheet is making a link between something they have seen and a construct they are interested in.

The added complexity of using video is that it provides for varying degrees of granularity with regards to both what can be made 'visible' and the complexity of the constructs that can be linked to what is then observed. In terms of visibility, the fact that video can be replayed any number of times and those viewing it can focus on the most subtle and minute of movements means that it can provide data on micro-interactions, such as subtle changes in facial movement, which would be difficult, if not impossible, to otherwise observe. At the same time, video can capture, over many weeks and months, the broad pattern of interactions within a given context, providing for macro levels of data. In a single project, the use of video allows a researcher to move from the micro to the macro level of analysis and to indent these levels one among another. Video therefore provides for differing degrees of granularity, not only in what is recorded but also in how it is analysed. It is this potential of video to allow for the indentation of differing levels of data, from the micro to the macro, that makes it possible to link it with complex theoretical constructs which go beyond what can be seen in a single frame or section of 'raw' video. Indenting the micro within the macro is important because, once researchers move away from making simple, direct linkages between what they are observing and what they are recording and start to look at more complex interactions, and the meaning these have for participants, they have to analyse not just the observed behaviour but also the context in which it takes place. This is because it is often the context, including the interactions that precede and follow a specific interaction, which gives it meaning for both the participant and the researcher. This movement between context and behaviour, and at points certain behaviours form the contexts for other behaviours and do so at increasingly finer levels of analysis, is the key to unlocking the 'non-visible' meanings within the video record.

As we will discuss later, many of the analytical processes within this modality are based around breaking video down into segments and then setting these within a series of contexts, across both time and space. It is this process of indenting specific interactions within multiple contexts that marks the movement between treating video as type (a) and type (b) data. The root of most criticisms we have experienced when showing video data to a research audience is their failure to recognise that video is often used as neither strictly a primary nor a secondary data source, but rather as a composite data source. By composite we mean that, not only can differing sections of the same video be used as primary and secondary data, and the same part of a video may well shift in status according to the focus, but that the highly layered nature of raw video and the indented nature of edited video mean that it offers an almost infinite degree of granularity. This degree of granularity means that varying forms of connection can be made between the video as data and the construct being researched, from a section of a single frame to the narrative of a social interaction constructed across several minutes of edited video. Within any series of indentations, micro aspects of an interaction captured on video can be given meaning by being placed within specific macro contexts. There is, therefore, no simple line that can be drawn between 'raw' and 'edited' video, because, as we discuss later, what is chosen to be filmed within a 'raw' sequence is equally as theoretically and culturally configured as any edited piece of video.

Video blurs the distinction between the processes of gathering information and generating data, and so it is perhaps unsurprising that criticisms arise when it is treated simplistically as either primary or secondary data. Researchers that treat it as a robust primary data source will want to 'see' the construct in the video. On the other hand, those who perpetually relegate video to secondary status for anything but the most basic of social interactions fail to recognise how it is possible to operationalise a construct within a multilayered video case study by indenting the micro within the macro. The strength of the divergent reactions we have received on showing our videos reveals to us as much about the ambiguous status of video within the research community as it does the lack of understanding about its potential as a data source and what constitutes an appropriate analytical process.

The status of video within the research community brings us to our second key issue, the extent to which it is treated as an objective data source. Our approach to video is no different from that to any other data source. Our position is that there is no completely 'objective' source of data; rather, there are data that are viewed, and treated, with a high degree of criticality and reflexivity, which means the researcher recognises the extent to which it is technically, theoretically and culturally laden, in contrast to data that are collected and handled with little recognition of these influences. Is video then affected by these influences in ways that distinguish it from other forms of data?

Let us deal with the technically 'laden' nature of video first of all: the issue of what effect video technology has on the nature of the data that can be recorded. We look at key issues involved in data collection in more detail in the following section, but the technology shapes video data in a number of subtle and significant ways, beyond the problems associated with filming. For example, the possibility of using multiple cameras gives researchers the potential of creating views of a situation that no one participant within a context would have access to. This technological 'feat' can shape the status given to the video data, in that it could potentially provide insights that could not have been obtained either by a single observer or by any participant in the context. As we discuss later in the section on analysis, video replay technology also allows for group or collective analysis. This process can not only help groups of researchers make clearer connections between data and the constructs they support, what Roth (2007) describes as a process of 'objectification', but in our terms supports the development of a shared critical subjectivity. This is because, as groups of researchers, or a mixed group of participants and researchers, watch the same piece of video, they can engage in group reflection and discussion as to what is occurring in it. Analytical processes such as collectively conducted interaction analysis (Jordan and Henderson, 1995) mean that video has the potential to move researchers on from concerns over inter-observer reliability to much deeper questions about the inter-subjective nature of their interpretations of others' interactions and the validity of such interpretations (Goldman-Segall, 1998).

Video is theoretically 'laden' in the sense that theory affects the type and range of data that need to be collected to explore the interaction or construct under study. It is common among researchers (Barren, 2007; Hall, 2000) who use video to stress that theory influences the process of data collection before even the camera is switched on, as decisions are made as to where to position the camera and what is to be filmed. In this sense though, video is little different from the process of 'boundarying' a case study (Winter, 1989), which is done by deciding when a social phenomenon stops and starts and what contexts and individuals need to be included in the data collection process. In contrast, Hall (2000) makes the case that, at least with regard to classroom videography, there are other potential theoretical possibilities. The first of these is the potential of video to 'stretch' the theoretical focus of the data collection process outside the boundaries of existing cases by the use of multiple video and audio data streams.

> By starting with multiple video and audio perspectives on activities that occur naturally in the workplace, we can do work at a theoretical level that stretches cognition (e.g. inference, calculation, teaching, learning) over people, things, and space in new and interesting ways.
>
> (Hall, 2000, p. 5)

Hall puts forward the case that video is not just theoretically laden but also theoretically enabling. It can support the researcher in terms of scope, by 'stretching' or supporting the exploration of a social interaction across differing spaces and interactions from a range of perspectives and at different degrees of granularity.

We have already discussed the strong cultural 'status' of video in society and how it affects participants, but does it have an equivalent effect on how researchers view it as data and how it can be used in their research? Video is culturally 'laden' on a number of levels. First, cultural norms affect judgements about the visual 'veracity' of images, the tendency to believe that what is captured on film represents what actually happened. Although researchers are, to a degree, likely to be able to stand outside this particular cultural influence in terms of how they themselves view video materials, it does influence how research subjects respond. This affects everything, from the way in which individuals react to the presence of a video camera to the 'performances' they may give in front of it. Second, it may be reflected in the relative status given to video within a range of other data. Video data might be not handled with the same degree of criticality as other forms of data. Third, it can affect the analysis of raw video data. We have all consumed video and films in their various forms, and assimilated their genres, their symbolism and conceits, and their narrative structure. Because we are so used to viewing edited video, which is consciously designed to convey a certain message or evoke a response in the viewer, when viewing 'raw' observational video it is almost impossible to avoid overlaying this form of data with narrative structures and nuances. This issue is made all the more problematic when those within the video appear to be 'acting out' recognisable narratives. The final cultural influence arises out of concerns over the visual, or what might now be more commonly called the digital, identities of individuals (Palfrey and Gasser, 2008). Concerns about the abuse and manipulation of video imagery, issues over privacy brought about by the widespread use of CCTV, and questions of retention of visual data have heightened sensitivities among participants and researchers alike. This has affected the whole video process, from collection through to storage. These are concerns that, paradoxically, both limit the usage of video while giving it even greater status, as it becomes more demanding to extract.

The key point here is that, taken in isolation, technical, theoretical and cultural factors would seem to have no more influence on video than any other form of data. What does seem to distinguish it is that these may interact in quite dramatic ways in the case of video, and that such interactions challenge the degree to which it is critically assessed as data.

What shapes the kind of video materials we extract from any situation?

Just as the interaction between technical, cultural and theoretical factors shape the status we give to video as data, they also affect what is extracted from any given situation. In this section, we unashamedly forefront the technical issues as, in our experience, if these are not dealt with then the video that is taken from a situation is of such poor quality that the influence of the other factors becomes minimal. Technically speaking, video recording is both a craft that needs to be learned and a rapidly evolving technology that needs to be understood. The craft knowledge associated with video is hard won, based on failures as much as successes, and difficult to put down on paper. On the other hand, it is enduring and, in the main, commonsensical once you are clear about what is important. In contrast, information about the technology is abundant – available on numerous blogs and forums – but often impenetrable to the novice and relatively transient. In this section, we therefore concentrate upon the craft knowledge we have built up in nearly twenty years of working with video. If you need advice about the technology, ask a technician or enthusiast, but keep in mind two caveats. First, work with established technology, not the 'next coming thing', even if it is claimed to be superior. In the end, marginal improvements are not as important as working with a robust technical platform that requires little expertise and has had the glitches ironed out. Second, do not get seduced into a spiral of ever-increasing quality and production values, because you are not making a high-end art movie and you need to focus on ease of use and capturing the interactions you want to focus on.

Trying to capture certain social interaction on video and working in particular contexts can present unique technical challenges, but in our experience there are a few constant issues that researchers need to be aware of. Here we focus on three:

- pictures go where you put them, but sound goes everywhere;
- following and framing the action;
- habituation, hides and hidden cameras.

'Pictures go where you put them, but sound goes everywhere'

This was a memorable lament of a video technician we were working with during the IPSUP project, which involved us in live satellite broadcasting across numerous sites in Europe. As we struggled with feedback howling around the studio speakers, we were provided with a clear lesson about the very different characteristics of sound versus pictures. In terms of collecting video materials, the differences mean that where you point the camera will be where your pictures will come from, but, on the other hand, sound can be picked up from almost anywhere, from behind the camera, echoing off surfaces that surround it, and even floating in from outside the building you are filming in. These differing characteristics mean that, in most cases, capturing good sound is far more difficult than obtaining clear pictures. This means that, if sound is important in your research, you will probably need to put more resource and effort into it than you first imagined.

First, let's start with equipment, and more specifically microphones. The ones that are on most small video cameras are only going to be adequate if you are recording in a quiet space, with subjects who are facing the camera. If this is not the case, then you need to consider one of the other types of commonly available microphone, and which one you choose will depend on where and how many people you want to record. If you want to focus on one person and the interactions they have with others, then you can use a small clip microphone attached to their clothing, similar to those used by television presenters. These are relatively cheap, and, if your subject is remaining still, you can simply connect the microphone to the camera by the use of a long lead. It is more likely, though, that you will want to pick up their conversations as they move around. Here, you have two options. First, you can use a wireless microphone. This consists of a sender unit, which the subject wears and is attached to the microphone transmitting a signal to a receiver unit, which plugs into the camera. Once very expensive, simple wireless microphone set-ups are now relatively cheap and easy to use, as long as you only want to capture the conversations of one or two people; once it gets beyond this, it can get costly, as more complex multichannel receivers are required. There is also the problem that subjects have to wear what can be a relatively bulky sender unit, which may be difficult to accommodate on, or in, their clothing, and so you might have to warn them and experiment with this. For an interesting discussion of some of the practical limitations of using wireless microphones with video while filming schoolchildren, see Tapper and Boulton (2002). The other option is to connect the clip microphone to a small digital recorder, many of which are half the size of the average mobile phone. These are cheap, can run for long periods of time on small batteries and can be carried easily. The downside is that you will need to have the technical ability to reconnect the audio to the video and so need to be able to use a basic video-editing package on your computer.

By using one of these packages, you can insert the sound recording from the digital recorder as an additional audio track and synchronise it with the pictures. This is a simple process, but you might want to consult a technician about which recorder and which software package to use, as there are various forms of digital sound file. If you choose a digital recorder that saves the audio track in an obscure or difficult format that cannot be handled easily by your video-editing package, then it can quickly become frustrating.

More often than not, within classroom videography, what you are trying to capture are the ongoing interactions between groups of pupils and the class teacher. In these cases, you are trying to record their conversations against a background of general classroom hubbub. In these situations, some form of boundary or plate microphone is best. By placing one of these omnidirectional microphones on a table at the centre of a group, the sound waves that pass over it are picked up. For the best effects, it is advisable to raise the microphone slightly above table level, which also reduces the noise of the inevitable knocks and thumps that arise from pupils working. The closer the group sits together around the microphone, the more likely they will form a barrier to the external noises from the rest of the class. Again, a radio microphone set-up could be used, otherwise a long cable will need to be attached and carefully taped down to the classroom floor to avoid it becoming a trip hazard. The interactions between the group and the teacher can either be picked up by the boundary microphone or may be supplemented by giving the teacher a clip microphone to wear. In these instances, the two sound-tracks will need to be combined.

The final form of microphone is a directional microphone, which can be placed at a distance and targeted at an individual or group. We have never found the need to use these within a classroom, as we have always found a combination of boundary and clip microphones to be sufficient, and the high levels of background noise tend to mitigate the use of all but the most expensive directional microphones. If, however, you are trying to gather sound from interactions at a distance and where there is limited background noise they may be useful.

In general, sound quality is often the weak link in generating a high-quality video record. Researchers need to allocate as much of their thinking and resources to this issue as to they do to collecting a good visual record. If you cannot afford a radio microphone set-up, then a good selection of cables will also be important, and do not forget to buy plenty of tape to secure the cables to the floor. The final point is make sure you have a good pair of headphones, so that you can check sound levels off the camera as the filming takes place. There is nothing more frustrating than to have worked all day capturing the right pictures, only to find on playback that you haven't picked up the sound.

Following and framing the action

Issues of how we follow and frame a social interaction are probably the point at which it is most apparent how theoretical and practical issues come together. In classroom videography, how we define teaching and where we look for learning are highly influential in what we film and the perspectives adopted. To help us think through how we will follow an interaction, the device we have most frequently used in our own work has been a rough shooting schedule, based on 'boundarying' the social interaction we are studying. To do this, we build a three-dimensional space that defines who, what, where and when we film. We define this space by the use of three separate dimensions illustrated in Figure 2.1.

The temporal dimension asks you to consider when the interaction you are interested in begins and ends. Although this might seem obvious in the first instance, it often changes as the research develops. In our own work

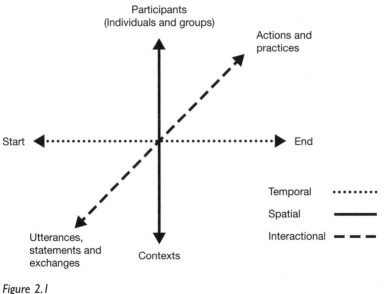

Figure 2.1
Who, what,
where and when
to film

within classrooms, we have often had to extend our video recording of a specific learning episode beyond the formal boundaries of a lesson and follow it over a number of weeks. The spatial dimension asks you to consider which individuals and groups over which contexts need to be filmed in order to capture the social interaction you are interested in. In classroom videography, it might involve filming, not only pupils and their teacher within the class-room, but also the interactions of pupils with peers outside in the playground, or at home with their parents, or teachers planning together or assessing pupils' work. The final dimension is interactional and is concerned with how you have operationalised or problematised the interaction you are interested in. This is, therefore, concerned with how you have conceptualised the inter-action you are interested in and translated this into behaviours and practice, forms of talk and the other exchanges that occur between participants. As with all projects, the degree of sophistication of how interactions are initially operationalised will vary owing to the current levels of understanding of it and how well it has been theorised. All these dimensions are likely to develop over the length of a project, and, at some point, the boundaries will have to be delimited, as they could potentially carry on expanding.

Once you have 'bounded' the interaction you are interested in, you will have created a rough shooting schedule, and so you should be much clearer about who, what, where and when you need to be filming. This is important, because simply putting up a camera and pressing the record button may seem an easier option, but often results in hours of recordings that have to be trawled through for a few relevant moments. This is time consuming and can result in the well-known phenomenon of 'death by data', in which the researcher drowns in a sea of data, and the project grinds to a halt. Having decided how you will follow the interaction, you now need to move on to consider how you will frame it.

Framing an interaction requires you to operate at a much more refined level, as it means thinking through from which perspective, or perspectives, you need to capture the interaction. In our own research in classroom videography, this often involves us in a multiple-camera set-up. For example, we might use one camera at the back of the classroom, set on a wide angle to record the general flow of interactions around the room and to record the teacher when they are talking to the whole class. We might then have a second camera that is focused in on one group of students, to capture the interactions among themselves and how they react to any teacher input. We have used this set-up when trying to look at the role of teachers in supporting collaborative group work, as it illustrated how the group operated before the teacher came over to discuss with them how they were doing, the interactions of the teacher with them, and how, and if, the group changed as a result of the input of the teacher. Even a two-camera set-up cannot fully capture the details of these interactions between the group and the teacher. Ideally, in addition to the wide-angle camera on the whole class, we would want two different camera angles on the group, a camera pointing into the group, but set back slightly, to capture their interactions and responses when the teacher came over to talk to them, and one pointing out from the group and towards the teacher, in order to capture the perspective of the pupils on input. One possible way round this is for the researcher to be in the room, using a hand-held camera to try and ensure they capture the outward-looking perspective by shooting from behind the group as they pay attention to the teacher. The obvious issue here, which we discuss in the next section, is the impact of a researcher wandering around with a video camera on pupils and teacher alike.

Framing requires the researcher to consider perspectives and, therefore, to think in three dimensions, and we are often struck by how novice researchers simply assume the camera will do all the work and somehow capture all the nuances they are after. Failing to consider perspective in detail means that novices are often disappointed that all they have managed to come away with are shots of the backs of people, or an empty screen as individuals have moved out of the frame. In part, the lack of attention of novices to this issue is because we are so culturally used to watching films and television programmes in which details of facial movements and the nuances of interactions seem to be effortlessly captured. Part of the 'magic' of these video materials is that we remain unaware of the multiple camera angles and repeated set-ups that have been used to achieve this effect. There are no simple solutions to properly framing an interaction, but there are a number of things we can do to both sensitise ourselves to the problem and consider the best technical response to the issue.

Following and framing are the major technical issues faced in capturing an adequate video record. As such, they also reflect the influence of the theoretical construction of the interaction by the researcher and the media culture that surrounds them. Our experiences have taught us that we need to adopt a flexible approach to setting boundaries, but the benefits of starting with too narrow a focus and then expanding it massively outweigh the problems associated with too broad a focus that results in collecting and viewing hours of irrelevant video materials.

As we have tended to work in an extractive mode, mainly in classroom environments, we have had to work within the confines of these sometimes chaotic natural settings. Another approach to dealing with the issues of following and framing is to create artificial situations that make the collection of video data much easier. There is a long history of using one-way mirrors and settings that are almost akin to stage sets, in order to provide more controlled conditions for filming (Rothbart *et al.*, 1971). Such approaches are often unfeasible or out of the reach of researchers who do not have extensive budgets. There is, though, no reason why a certain amount of 'stage-setting' cannot be undertaken by any researcher. This might be as simple as reorientating a table and making sure that, at least initially, chairs are best positioned to allow for a single camera to capture the interactions of individuals. More elaborate stage-dressing might involve the construction of simple 'sets' by arranging existing furniture and lighting.

Habituation, hides and hidden cameras

As we have already mentioned, the presence of a video camera may encourage individuals to 'act out', as they move into a kind of performance mode. In other situations, a camera might not just subvert what occurs between individuals, but so constrain them as to make 'normal' interactions impossible. Here, the researcher can draw on the wealth of experience of wildlife photographers who set out to capture animals in their natural habitats.

The first tool of the wildlife photographer is the fact that most animals will quickly become habituated to the presence of a remotely controlled, static camera. Although the habituation response is less strong within human beings, it can be used to good effect. In our own work within classrooms, we would often set up the cameras in the classrooms some weeks before actual filming would begin. Taping over the red recording lights at the front of the camera also meant no one in the classroom was aware when actual recording was taking place. Placing microphones on several tables also obscured which group was being filmed. Tapper and Boulton (2002) made up a series of 'dummy' radio microphones, so that no child was aware of who was being filmed. Once the participants seem to have become unaware of the camera, then filming can begin, with the camera being activated using a remote.

The second tool available to the wildlife photographer is the hide, a device that allows them to observe animals close up without being noticed by the animals and means they only need to take the specific shots they want. We have never gone to the lengths of actually building a hide in a classroom, but video technology does allow you to observe others without being physically in the same space. All that is required is a camera with a video and audio out, a long length of cable to connect to a monitor and a space outside the classroom. This we have found an easier proposition in primary or first schools, because they tend to have more open-plan layouts, with various areas in which the researcher can set up the monitor. Now, the researcher can observe the classroom and only record those interactions they are interested in. Where it is impossible to work outside the classroom, or a static camera is unlikely to capture the interaction, then the researcher will need to work in the classroom. 'Hiding' in such an environment is difficult, but you can make yourself less obtrusive by following some simple rules. If possible, establish yourself in the classroom without a camera – often we work as classroom assistants. Next, take in the camera and try filming with the camera on your lap, using the fold-out screen; this is far less obtrusive than filming through the eyepiece. It does take practice, but we would normally be found sitting at the edge of the classroom filming with the camera on our laps, which makes it unclear who we are focusing on, or even if the camera is recording. Finally, we try and position ourselves out of the direct eyeline of the group and avoid coming between the group and where the teacher normally addresses the whole class.

The final tool is the hidden camera, by which we do not mean covert filming, as, in our work, participants are always kept fully informed. Cameras can be concealed by a variety of means, on top of cupboards or within storage units; in one of our own projects, we included a camera in a classroom display about film and media. Increasingly, small cameras are built into, or can be attached to, phones and computers, and these can provide additional angles. For example, when we wanted to capture how pupils collaborated when using a computer, we used the inbuilt camera on the computer to provide an additional viewpoint, as it 'looked out', and then placed another camera pointing into the group from behind, which 'looked in' at them, giving an almost 360° view of the group.

Does video require a different approach to analysis?

In general, descriptions of the differing approaches to video analysis are more of a reflection of the origins and theoretical dispositions of individual researchers than they are shaped by the nature of video as data. There are two exceptions to this rule. The first involves detailed studies of micro social interaction, such as those described within interactional ethnography (Green *et al.*, 2007), as against those that approach edited video more as a form of semiotic resource open to differing layers of discourse analysis (Rose, 2008). These represent two very different extremes. At the one end, it is the technology that dominates, allowing as it does for the most fine-grained of analysis.

> The analysis of social interaction is foundational to the use of videotape in learning research, because it has consistently delivered on a promise: that if looked at carefully enough, *where carefully means an hour of transcription and analysis per second of videotape*, every behaviour, no matter how bizarre, or seemingly nonresponsive, is part of a coherent string of behaviours developed across persons and across time, by some mix of agreements, contrasts, and contradictions in tune with the demands of the moment.
>
> (Goldman and McDermott, 2007 p. 110,
> emphasis added)

At the other end, it is the cultural ubiquity and power of film that mean every angle and perspective in a video can be imbued with some form of cultural meaning. Between these two extremes lies a broad field that ranges from those who adopt an approach akin to those used in the content analysis of written documents (Rose, 2008) to those who use approaches familiar to those involved in case study research (Walker, 2002).

So, does video require a different approach to analysis? The straightforward answer is no. In the majority of cases, the analysis of video follows a similar process to that used in dealing with any other form of data. The overall approach will be based on the overarching theoretical framework that shapes the research; it is more than likely it will involve the same stages and the application of similar analytical rules or principles for how to move from 'data' to findings. The main challenges arise because of the nature of the data themselves and the problems and potentials presented by the technology. In this section, therefore, we do not intend to go into all the possible ways in which video data might be handled in the extractive mode. Instead, we will wrap around well-established approaches our own interpretation of how video analyses might differ from more established ways of working.

It is something of a cliché that analysis is not a stage in qualitative research but a strand that runs through it. In the case of video, it is worth reminding ourselves of the need to keep up the analysis throughout the project, because the richness of video makes it more likely that researchers will carry on filming without reviewing what has already been captured. The most basic level of ongoing analysis needed is logging the video collected. In our own

Table 2.1 An outline logging sheet

Tape/File name	In	Out	Brief description	Analytical note
22.3.10 Parkside Cam 1	00.00	02.30	Introduction to the session by class teacher	
	2.30	3.15	Teacher deals with requests from pupils for resources	
	3.15	4.00	Teacher approaches group and discusses their understanding of task	

projects, we do this as soon as possible after we have finished filming. We go through each tape or file and make a brief record of what it contains. These logging sheets will vary in detail, depending upon what stage we are at in the project. Early on, we might be relatively unsure as to what we are looking for, and our logging sheet will reflect this by only breaking the video down into the main phases of activity, or what appear to be relatively natural sequences. So, on the logging sheet (Table 2.1), we would put times 'in' and 'out' to mark out the section. This will be drawn either from the time and date codes on the camera or on the editing software if we are putting the video straight onto a computer as it comes in. If you are intending to have an edited version of the raw video created by someone else, you might wish to use some form of time code here, so that they are sure which edits you want, and no confusion arises as you move between different playback and editing machines.

Later on, as we become clearer about what we are looking for, then these sections might become more finely tuned, possibly smaller in size, with more analytical notes. Logging the video as it comes in is not just a technical archiving process; it is the beginning of the formalised analysis process. It does two things that are analytically powerful. First, it provides the researcher with an overview of the data as they come in, which helps the researcher pick up on patterns and contradictions they find interesting – hence, we have a column for analytical notes in our coding sheets. The second thing it does is help with data management and reduction. As areas of interest emerge in later recordings, these logging sheets help with finding sections previously skimmed over, which can now undergo more in-depth analysis. In the later stages, when even finer-grained analysis is required, the sheets help the researcher draw together the most relevant sections. This cuts down considerably the amount of time spent running backward and forward through masses of irrelevant video.

After the logging-in process has been completed, the video analysis moves from being an open to a more structured process (Collier, 2001; Erickson 1982). The logging-in process is little more than an attempt to break the video down into what appear to be relatively 'natural' sections. Now, these sections will be reviewed using either an emergent or a pre-existing analytical framework. In some instances, projects start off with a highly structured logging schedule that might have additional columns to allow for the tracking of individuals through various recordings or provide help in mapping the flow of interactions within a setting. For those researchers for whom the frequency of events is important, then more attention has to be paid to how the video record is segmented, as how it is divided up will determine the eventual number of counts made.

Defining units of analysis is important in all instances where the researcher wants to make a series of comparative analyses between the same types of interaction. In these cases, it is important to apply theoretical constructs consistently in terms of both identifying and segmenting relevant sections and then analysing these. Here, Angelillo *et al.* (2007) offer sound advice on how to segment a video record:

> To determine the length of segments for a particular study, we consider the pace of the activities, the nature of the coding categories, and the 'mental load' of the coder. A stretch of a video segment should not be so long that it contains too many of the target events or creates a burden for remembering the details necessary for coding: it should not be so short that it is difficult to achieve an understanding of the meaning of the participants' actions.
>
> (Angelillo *et al.*, 2007, p. 204)

To lessen this load, we have developed a technique based upon the facility in most video-editing software to create multiple tracks of video. Our approach is to import the video being analysed into the program and have this as the top or first track. We then use the logging sheet to identify those sections that are most relevant. These are put onto the second track.

We then go through these sections and identify the interactions we are interested in, and these become the third, final track. We then export just this track and save the whole project with all the video, just in case we need to go back and look at previously disregarded sections. We save the key extracts and combine them with other recordings to make a composite analysis DVD, which can then be copied and played back though multiple computers. This means that we now have the ability to make a series of comparative analyses across a range of similar interactions, watching them either simultaneously or sequentially. We can even parcel out the task of analysis, giving different researchers the same extracts, and compare their analyses together as a group.

At this point, one can quickly enter a 'can't see the wood for the trees' situation, in which a focus on ever more specific segments means that they become decontextualised and so lose a degree of their meaning. Here, there is a need to play analytically with the layered nature of video data. This might involve the reinsertion of segments into the elements that surround them, a process made relatively easy by the use of the layered analysis into differing video tracks described earlier. These cycles of moving within and between layers of video data form a recursive process that allows both for the use of grounded approaches as well as the refinement of pre-existing analytical frameworks. It is during these recursive cycles that the researcher will apply the core analytical techniques and approaches appropriate to his or her research tradition. There are various accounts of these methods and principles spread throughout the literature on video analysis. They might involve forms of phenomenological bracketing in order to make unfamiliar everyday interaction, or the application of principles such as concurrence, absence, consistency and ambiguity to understand social structures, or the movement between micro, meso and macro levels of social analysis (Erickson, 1982).

Within these recursive cycles, researchers are moving the visual data through a number of levels of analysis. At the primary analytical level, they are treating video as representing differing forms of behavioural sequences, key interactions between collectivities and groups, or expressions of societal, cultural or ideological norms. At this level, the main analytical activity is the operationalisation, identification and categorisation of the video data in order to link them to key constructs, or units of meaning, within the existing or emergent analytical frameworks devised. The second analytical level is more interpretive, with the researcher taking the elements previously identified and embedding them within broader sequences of interactions, looking for them in different contexts, or focusing on specific aspects of the sequences. This invokes a series of 'part and whole' analytical movements, the setting and resetting of sequences of video in broader and narrower flows of activities, and comparisons between differing sequences that involve the researcher in both 'vertical' and 'horizontal' coding. What is 'interpretational' about this level of analysis will depend upon the overall aim of the research. It may be concerned with the meaning that interactions have for the subjects involved within them, or the 'meaningfulness' they generate within social interactions. In most cases, it involves the researcher in another level of analysis, which is a process of reinterpretation and rearticulation of the subjective experience of those on the video. The main analytical activities here are deductive and inductive processes that allow for the application of an existing theoretical framework to a sequence of video, or for the emergence of new frameworks and constructs. The final analytical level is that of extrapolation, which again will take a variety of terms, depending upon the nature of the research project. The extrapolation may be mainly theoretical in nature, allowing the researcher, by reference to broader organisational or social structures, to explain how the meaningfulness of interactions is sustained and brought about across a range of contexts. When the extrapolation is more empirical in nature, it can become the search for broader social patterns and generalisations that typify certain interactions, or identify what is universal (Elliot, 2006) or distinct about a specific case. The main analytical activities here range from theoretical hypothesising to the postulation of fuzzy generalisations and statistical analysis of patterns across a sample.

Researchers tend to discuss analysis as operating across differing levels, demarcated by the application of increasingly more abstract levels of theory. Our own approach is to treat these levels as three interacting cogs that drive forward the analytical process. Within a particular research tradition, whatever the analytical techniques or tools used, or the levels that are gone through, the approach to video data does not appear to be that distinct from other forms of analysis data. What we have found to be unique about video data, and what drew us as a research group into their use, was the way in which these techniques and principles could be applied collectively.

Our engagement with video in research came about when we were a group of new researchers who shared a set of interconnected rooms in a traditional university that assumed that we would each sit, monk-like, in them. Instead, we adapted one room for our day-to-day work, converted another for meetings and dedicated the third as a quiet room for writing and analysis. As two of us were already involved in different projects using video, we also set up a television and VCR so that we could review what we had recently filmed. Although the room was used to write reports, no one ever played their audiotapes in this quiet room, but increasingly we would sit around and look at each other's videos. Possibly, as a generation, we had lost the tradition of a family sitting around a wireless listening together and so feel less able to jointly analyse audio data, but culturally we are all familiar and comfortable with watching television with others. These sessions began informally, as we passed one or other and just joined in. This was possible because the tapes were so rich a source of data we could absorb the context and purpose of each other's research more easily and so offer meaningful interpretations and observations. The room had also been set out to make video analysis more comfortable, with a small settee that allowed two people to watch together. From these informal sessions, we began to appreciate the ability of video to stimulate shared analysis, initially from very different perspectives. We then began to build such sessions more formally into new projects. It was only later that we realised that others had begun to understand and explore the potential of collective analysis of video.

Partially because of these early experiences, we are strong advocates of collective analysis and feel it should be a way in which video is treated differently to other data sources. Our belief is based on our own observations and reflections on the benefits of turning what is often an individual process, based on the written word, into one that is collective and based on dialogue. The main benefits we found were that it improved, not only the specificity of the constructs being used to analyse the tapes, but also how these were operationalised; it gave a degree of triangulation to our analyses, as we debated the differences and similarities between different episodes; and, finally and most importantly, it was a creative and highly motivating process. Other researchers have used collective analysis to improve the 'objectivity' of video analysis (Roth, 2007) and to improve the reading across of multiple instances (Rogoff et al., 1993). Our own approach has been to see it as improving the quality of the critical subjectivity being applied to a study, rather than an attempt to reach some form of consensual 'truth' as to what the video has captured.

What are the key issues about using video to show your findings?

Tales of technical problems and unexpected audience responses to video-based presentations are part of the folklore of researchers who work with video. Technical problems arise from the range of video formats in existence, the instability of some of the video platforms, especially those that are web-based, and the lack of consideration many academic organisations give to presenting visual data. The potential of video to evoke vehement and often contradictory responses from members of an audience is testament to its cultural power, its somewhat ambiguous status as data and its potential to evoke comparisons across very different contexts and experiences.

It used to be the case that the greatest technical issues we faced arose because of the hardware required to play back differing types of videotape. Now, the major problem in this digital age is a software one, and whether the format of the video files are compatible with the most ubiquitous players such as Quicktime and Windows Media Player, or whether DVDs and CD-ROMs will run on different players. Our approach to these problems tends to be a belt and braces one. We not only use readily available freeware from the Internet to produce different versions of our media that are compatible with the more common players, we also still take our own computers to ensure that we can play our DVDs effectively. Dealing with the technical issues associated with showing video is mainly a question of good preparation and having a big bag in which to carry speakers, cables and your computer. Dealing with the variability of audience reactions is far more about understanding the psychology of viewing visual images and their potential to evoke strong visual memories.

To a lesser or greater extent, we all suffer from selective attention. That is, what we focus on depends upon our own interests and preconceptions. Video is such a rich data source that it is particularly vulnerable to individuals focusing on specific aspects, which have little relevance to your analysis, and then reinterpreting these in the light of their own interests and experiences. Video materials, as we discuss in the section on video within a reflective research modality, can also act as powerful triggers, stimulating recollections of past events. Our visual memories tend to be narrative in form, often incomplete, but from very specific personal perspectives. Within any given audience, a well-constructed piece of video has the potential to evoke a range of recollections that retain some of their original emotional and cognitive power. The phenomenon of selective attention, combined with the nature of visual memory, lies at the heart of the problem that, no mind how consciously we aim for a specific response from an audience by the conscientious selection, careful editing and detailed verbal introduction to a video, it is still likely to generate very eclectic responses. If you want to assess the strength of this phenomenon, take a short video clip of an individual or group talking and show it to an audience, with minimal introduction. Stop the video after, say, fifteen seconds and ask the audience what they can tell you about those involved. We are always struck by, not only the willingness of individuals to offer interpretations after such a short exposure, but also how detailed they often are.

We started off this chapter with the metaphor of the sports replay and have ended up with a brief discussion of the psychology of visual perception and cognition. To bring the two back together, we might consider that, when we are showing a video back to an audience, we have to recognise that they may not understand the sport being shown or may disagree with the commentators' and pundits' analysis. Maybe it is not that surprising that showing video in academic settings often generates such strange or vehement responses. We have argued that, when working with video in an extractive modality, it does not present any specific analytical challenges but quite a few technical ones, in terms of capturing the quality of data that will have meaning when they are removed from their context. In the next two chapters, this situation is almost inverted, as questions of analysis come to the fore.

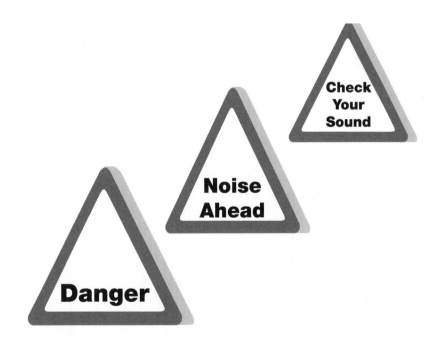

Chapter 3

Using video in a reflective mode

The use of video as a means of supporting participants to reflect predates the widespread interest across social science in notions of reflective practice and the reflective practitioner (Schön, 1987). There is, for example, a long history in visual anthropology of using pictures that are personal to participants to stimulate their reflections and recollections of past events, and this methodology has steadfastly tracked the available technologies, through 8 mm film to digital video (Banks, 2001). The current use of video in this modality tends to be dominated by differing forms of practitioner research, broadly aimed at understanding and improving professional practice. The pragmatic use of reflective theory has spread across different fields of applied research, from health and social services to the criminal justice system, and video has travelled with it.

Our own use of video in this modality was initially as a means of stimulating recall among teachers about their classroom practice (Hadfield, 1995). Since these initial attempts, we have moved on, in both our thinking and practice, to use it within a wide range of projects and particularly community consultations (Hadfield and Haw, 1997a). It could be argued that, to an extent, any project that uses video as part of the research process, from being a stimulus in a focus group to presenting its findings, is prompting others to reflect on what has been achieved. In this chapter, we focus on the research of others, as well as our own, that has used video explicitly to prompt reflection among research participants, whether they be practitioners or not, and that has not just a narrow pragmatic focus on improving practice.

The root metaphor

Our preferred root metaphor for thinking about how video is used in this modality is a development of probably the commonest metaphor for

reflection, that of an individual contemplating their image in a mirror. This is a useful starting point because it illuminates two aspects of reflection that are vital to grappling with the use of video in this modality. First, it picks up on the idea that reflection is a reflexive act, one that forms a connection between observer and image, particularly their own image, a connection that turns back on the observer and affects how they see, and what they see. As the observer views an image, how they perceive it changes, because of shifts in perspective, both physical and cognitive, directly brought about by the act of observation. Second, the metaphor suggests a degree of indeterminacy in the relationship between observer and image, symbolised in the metaphor by the physical space between the individual and the mirror. This space allows a range of external and internal phenomena to intervene. Externally, changes in the level of illumination affect what can be seen, while internally, as the observer draws on different memories, they might change their interpretations of what they see in their image. The observer can manipulate their perspective and view themselves from a different angle, or be manipulated by changes in the viewing context. There is a sense of the observer making and unmaking a range of connections between themselves and their image, made possible because of the persistence of the image in front of them and the impermanence of the changing relationship between them. These changes impact upon acts of perception and cognition, with acts of reflection at one level resulting in reflections at another.

Within this metaphor, reflection is an act of connection that is both reflexive and dialectical. There are notions of both distance and closeness in the metaphor of the observer and the image in the mirror. There is space to stand back and look at oneself 'in the round', while, at the same time, there is an opportunity to move towards the image and closely examine a particular aspect of one's features. The mirror provides both a persistent and 'changing' image because:

- it creates a reference point for the observer's existing judgements about themselves and their situations, because an apparently 'objective' image can be juxtaposed with their 'subjective' memory of themselves;
- it can make them both focally and peripherally aware of their own image and what surrounds it;
- it is a connection in which the observer can apply their memory, perceptual apparatus and cultural frameworks in support of a range of judgements;
- it is a situation in which the observer makes their own images an object of their subjectivity.

The individual contemplating his or her reflection in a mirror is a powerful root metaphor for thinking about the reflective use of video in social science research, as it highlights a number of key characteristics and potentials in this modality:

- Video can present various 'objective' images of the participant back to themselves, either self-generated or by others – who holds the mirror up to the observer?
- Video technology means that a wide range of participant activities, across a variety of contexts, can be reflected upon in various combinations – the mirror as a reflection of a changing self.
- Video allows an observer repeatedly to explore an image from different directions and varying proximities, thus allowing them to consciously shift their focus as they reflect – mirrors that can provide a full-length 360° image and detailed close-ups.

- The video image shown to participants can be designed so as to present alternative or contradictory 'images' of themselves and challenge their current conceptions – the distorted mirror that exaggerates or shrinks key features.
- Video can present to participants their own image set alongside those of others, which they can then reflect on individually or with others – the hall of mirrors.

The use of video within a reflective modality has grown out of a belief in the potential of moving visual images to prompt reflection among research participants. Video technology is seen as having enhanced this potential by providing more powerful stimuli containing richer images. Video is also a highly malleable medium and can be worked on by the researcher so as to focus the attention of the observer on areas of particular interest. It is also a very permissive medium that can be widely disseminated and shown on a range of technologies and so it can be used to prompt reflection across differing contexts and easily incorporated into a wide range of research methods.

The overarching rationale behind using video within this modality is to support participants engaging in different or deeper reflective acts. Research within this modality tends to operate under the broad umbrella of self-reflection and self-knowledge. Although the use of video may promote greater self-knowledge for the participant, whether this is a key aim of the research or treated as a 'spin-off' will depend upon the overall research paradigm it sits within. In many instances, the additional benefits that participants accrue from being more reflective are only of secondary interest to the researcher, as they might help keep them engaged with the research. If this is the case, then these researchers are mainly interested in reflection because it gives them greater access to how participants construct their actions and the contexts in which these occur. In contrast, for other researchers the main aim of their work is to generate greater self-awareness that leads to some form of ethical social change (Witteveen and Lie, 2009). These very different research agendas have a profound effect on how video is used within this modality.

We have structured the rest of this chapter around three interconnected questions:

- What kinds of reflection can the use of video support?
- How can researchers use video to engage participants in differing types of reflection?
- How do you design and use a video 'trigger tape' so that it supports participants to reflect?

What kinds of reflection can the use of video support?

Video has the potential to support almost any form of reflective activity. We would argue, however, that it is particularly useful when the research project involves one of the following two forms of reflective activity:

- when reflection is concerned with 'pausing' the flow between knowing and action, in order to study how the participant perceives the connections between the two;
- if reflection is about bringing together different aspects of participants' understanding of themselves, their actions and their contexts; here, reflection is a means of 'translating' different forms of understanding so that the participant can provide more integrated or detailed accounts.

There is a third form of reflective activity. This is in those instances where reflection helps the participant *attune* their reflective gaze towards areas that are generally ignored or omitted from consideration. These areas might be omitted for a variety of reasons, from the psychological to the cultural, and reflection as attunement involves participants refocusing and re-examining them. We have chosen to explore this more fully in the next chapter, on the role of video in projection and provocation.

These various types of reflective activity are linked by the idea of connection, between action and knowledge, aspects of self, and the individual and their context. Reflection is essentially concerned with participants either establishing new connections or changing existing ones. The notion of reflection as an act of connection runs through the literature of reflective practice. Take, for example, Van Manen's (1977) pivotal article, 'Linking ways of knowing with ways of being practical', which draws attention to the connection between forms of knowledge and action. One of our favourite quotations about reflection comes from Ornstein (1987) when describing the process of reflective writing and the construction of a journal entry:

> It contains a changeable conglomeration of different kinds of 'small minds' – fixed reactions, flexible thinking – and these different entities are temporarily employed – 'wheeled into consciousness' – and then usually discarded, returned to their place, after use.
>
> (Ornstein, 1987, p. 25, quoted in Holly, 1989, p. 76)

For us, video provides the researcher with the ability to create prompts and processes that will stimulate specific conglomerations of these 'small minds' of participants and 'wheel these into consciousness', where they can be connected and reconnected. This can be done by showing video materials that have been specifically edited to target various 'small minds', or it might involve participants in the process of making a video, where cycles of reflection and decision-making within filming and editing prompt them to consider, in depth, the issue that is the focus of the final video product. The primary utility of video in this modality is that it can support participants in making connections between disparate elements of their actions and practices, where other approaches would be likely to fail. For example, another popular reflective technique is journaling, but this requires a level of commitment or technical skills that certain participants do not possess. When used appropriately in this modality, video can both support participants through a process of reflection and capture the outcomes from it in a format that makes it relatively easy for researchers to apply their analytical and theoretical framework.

Reflection as a pause

Possibly the most basic change to an existing connection, and implicit within the idea of 'pausing for thought', is the idea that reflection involves a slowing down of what is occurring.

> When we stop to think – to reflect – we do so in order to take stock of something that has happened, in order to prepare ourselves for action, or (usually) to do both.
>
> (Kemmis, 1985, p. 141)

This pause might take place within an ongoing activity or during a recollection of what has happened. Descriptions of reflective phases in early action research projects (McNiff, 1988) and studies of experiential learning (Heron, 1985) constructed reflection as a 'pause', akin to a 'time out' from intense professional contexts, that aimed to help participants learn from their prior experiences.

> The validity of the reflection phase will in part be a function of how much reflection there is in relation to how much experience. Brief and cursory reflection upon deep and extended experience is not likely to yield up much truth-value; similarly with elaborate and prolonged refection upon a fleeting trace experience.
>
> (Heron, 1985, p. 131)

Here, the 'pause' is constructed as a break from experience, a quiet space, in which prior experiences can be recreated, processed and brought under greater scrutiny, away from the 'press' of their professional contexts.

The idea that reflection 'freezes the moment', making it available for further processing, found favour among the developers of early cognitivist theories of professional action and knowledge in the late 1970s and early 1980s. A central tenet of these early theories (Shulman and Elstein, 1975; Shavelson, 1976; Peterson and Clarke, 1978; Calderhead, 1981) was that practitioners, as information processors, were in danger of being over-whelmed by the flow of data from their surroundings and under the pressure of having to make numerous 'in-flight' decisions. Reflection was, therefore, popularly constructed as a means of helping practitioners 'pause' their highly dynamic and overwhelming relationship with their contexts and consider it in more detail.

The desire to 'pause' and give more consideration to this relationship gave rise to reflective techniques such as stimulated recall and thinking aloud (Clark, 1988), which, in their different ways, allowed for the recreation of the 'in-flight' decision-making of professionals. Relatively quickly, approaches such as stimulated recall moved on from the use of audio to video recordings as stimuli (Marland, 1984). Video provided the means to capture actions, interactions and contexts in a more cohesive manner than audio. Within a stimulated recall session, the participant is shown a video of an interaction they have taken part in and then prompted by the researchers to reflect on their role within it. This is normally done as soon after the episode as possible, in order to lessen the impact of memory loss or to avoid the participant reconstructing the event on the basis of what occurred after it. There is a range of protocols for how to use video within stimulated recall (Lyle, 2003). These tend to vary, depending upon the degree to which the research is concerned with developing the researcher's or the participant's understanding of the activity captured on video, the phenomena being reflected upon, and how the researcher constructs what the practitioner is actually accessing during the process of stimulated recall. Although protocols for the use of the video within stimulated recall differ, they basically consist of variations on a theme. The researcher and participant sit down together and review the video, and this session is recorded. These reviews are run with varying degrees of structure. More open reviews give the participant a much greater degree of control, with relatively little input from the researcher. So, for example, when using 'thinking aloud' procedures, the participant is simply prompted to provide a running commentary on what is being viewed. A more structured approach would be to use critical incidents (Butterfield *et al.*, 2005), where participants are asked to stop the video when they are conscious that something has differed from their established routines, or that feedback from others has significantly changed their view of what is occurring in the activity. The researcher would then probe around these incidents. Researchers from more cognitivist backgrounds might ask the participant to pause the video when they remember making a conscious decision about the situation and then unpack the decision-making process. The most structured approaches involve the researcher applying an analytical frame-work to the review and taking greater control. This would involve them in selecting the sections of the video to review, rather than just letting it 'roll'. They would then focus on specific interactions within these sections of the video, and the prompts used would be based upon their initial analysis of the situation being reviewed and would be derived from their own theoretical perspective.

In our own use of video-based stimulated recall, we initially adopted a critical-incidents approach, but with a pretty expansive view of what constituted an 'incident'. At one level, an incident within a video might be seen as critical because it revealed a break in the 'loop' between the under-standing by a participant of a situation, the actions they engaged in and the reactions of those around them. At other levels, the incident might be a disruption of participants' established routines that led to a moment of cognitive restructuring; it might be a flash of insight, the Gestaltist 'Aha' moment (Ollinger and Goel, 2010), where they suddenly developed a new insight into their actions or context. The inherent reflexivity of this form of analysis is particularly suited to video-based stimulated recall, because it allows the researcher and participant to move forward and backward through an incident. This supports the researcher in exploring, with the participant, their expectations about what was to occur next and what actually occurred. The level of this exploration is less about establishing the nature of participants' 'decisions', and more to do with exploring breakdowns and interruptions in their 'scripts' and moments of insight.

In our approach to stimulated recall, video is useful, not because it freezes the moments between knowledge and action, but because it allows for a more detailed study of the disruptions and discontinuities that participants notice in their reflexive relationships with others involved in the activity. It also has the potential to view these disruptions and discontinuities from multiple perspectives by getting others involved in the activity to review the video. Our approach is based on one of the key constructs of reflective theory, the reflexive 'feedback loop' between individuals and their contexts (Winter, 1989). We have developed the original idea by adopting a more expansive notion of the nature of these loops and the frameworks or scripts used by participants to construct them and interpret the 'feedback'.

In more recent theories, the idea of reflection as a pause has fallen out of favour, as theorists have sought to establish reflection as dynamic and interactive with practice and wider social discourses (Griffiths and Tann, 1992). There are, however, echoes of it in the idea of isolating aspects of past experience within narrative research (Cole and Knowles, 1993). Here, researchers have used participant-produced videos to pause the flow of their biographical accounts so as to bracket aspects of their experiences during the creation of their narratives. Video offers narrative researchers a means of pausing, reframing and re-storying individual biographies, especially when combined within multimedia formats (Kwan and Ding, 2008).

The image of the practitioner as someone having to deal with multiple demands and dealing with limited and vague feedback is an enduring one. It means that reflection continues to be associated with the idea of a break or 'pause' from this pressure. This has meant that video is still popular with researchers looking at professional practice who want to slow down or freeze the connections participants make with their 'reality' and actions. They simply need to keep in mind that a 'pause' is not just a condition for reflection, but is an act of reflection in which the participant connects and reconnects aspects of what they were doing in a particular event. When this reflective act is supported by video, they need to be clear about the distinction between the types of connection made within the actual action and the nature of the connections that reviewing a video is likely to prompt.

Reflection as an act of translation

Reflection as an act of translation operates across a broader spectrum of connections than those considered in the previous section. Here, we are not just concerned about researching the relationship between participants' actions, but are operating at the wider level of connecting various aspects of their 'architecture of self' (Pinar, 1988). This means connecting aspects of differing forms of knowledge, from the procedural to the declarative, and linking these with their value positions, moral frameworks, emotions and personal beliefs. It therefore draws together the personal and professional, the contextual and the universal, a form of reflection that encompasses research on identity, professional or otherwise, and its social construction.

The notion of translation is based on the idea that an individual's sense of self, of their identity, is essentially fragmented. Explanations of the nature and causes of this fragmentation will vary from one research tradition to another. In our own work, we have adopted slightly different constructions, but, when working with professionals, we have tended to theorise it as arising from the ways in which they build up their knowledge base and identities over long periods of time and from a variety of sources. This resultant fragmented understanding of a particular professional phenomenon comes about because it exists in differing forms and with various degrees of tacitness. Individuals' self-awareness of their fragmented identities varies, resulting in some professionals being able to articulate the contradictory nature of their actions and understandings, whereas others fail to recognise their shifts and inconsistencies. This is because, as Van Manen (1995) discusses, if we accept the notion of a fragmented self, then to a degree this relies upon a 'split awareness of self'. Van Manen created the image of the 'schizophrenic' professional, who is, to a lesser or greater extent, aware of different aspects of themselves, with certain aspects involved in almost independent dialogues.

> A phenomenology of tactful action may reveal several styles of intuitive practice: from acting in a largely self-forgetful manner to a kind of running inner speech that the interior eye of the ego maintains with the self. This split awareness of self manifests itself as a kind of natural schizophrenia, whereby one part of the self somehow dialogues with the other part.
>
> (Van Manen, 1995, p. 41)

If we wish to encourage quite a deep level of reflection among small numbers of participants about their fragmented identities, then we involve them in the process of video production. The process of producing a video can, if structured properly, allow participants to go through cycles of reflection that range across differing aspects of their understandings and touch upon fragments of their professional self. The basic processes involved in creating a video, from initial decisions about its focus, through who and what to film, to the final editing process, all present opportunities for reflection and insight that, if handled sensitively and structured properly by the researcher, can become a means of exploring and articulating aspects of their identities. It was this approach to reflective work with practitioners that led us down the path of using the process of video production itself as a central part of our approach to data generation. Over the years, this has also involved us in an increasing use of participatory approaches when using video. We discuss this more fully in Chapter 5. In this approach, the video product becomes increasingly less important as data because it represents only the tip of a layered data generation process, consisting of multiple moments of reflection and numerous 'conversations' about its development with participants, which we systematically record and analyse.

If we were concerned with trying to prompt more superficial levels of reflection across larger numbers of participants, then we tended to show them a 'trigger tape' and process their reactions. In the early stages of our use of video in this modality (Hadfield and Haw, 1997a), we developed the idea of a 'trigger tape'. This was an edited video designed to act as a prompt, or trigger, to support participants in reflecting upon specific issues and actions. A trigger video is designed to do this by focusing the reflections of participants on certain connections in specific ways. This is done by careful selection of what the trigger contains, how it is edited and how it is used with participants. These types of trigger tape are designed to be akin to 'visual Rosetta stones'. That is, they need to contain elements that represent, literally or symbolically, the fragmented aspects of the practitioners' professional understanding of an issue. This meant building trigger tapes that captured the contradictory nature of their views, highlighted tensions and presented back to them differing ways of engaging with an issue, from the moral to the emotional. Building in this range of elements is important, because reflection is not a singular act of translation.

When participants view a trigger tape, we are hoping that it stimulates several 'small minds' within their overall identities. These small minds contain their own little cohesive clusters of knowledge, cultural rules and moral imperatives that are, to varying degrees, integrated with other 'small minds'. Reflection helps these differing 'small minds' talk to each other by supporting a range of translations to take place. Cognitively, implicit understandings in different 'minds' are dragged to the surface where they can be consciously considered. Morally, the nature of a certain dilemma inherent in adopting a particular position is mapped out using rules and imperatives drawn from a variety of once-separated minds. Some of these dialogues may be therapeutic, as participants unravel the contradictions that have arisen in their under-standings and how these are sustained. The design of this kind of trigger video and the structuring of the discussion that surrounds it are therefore based on the recognition of both the fragmented nature of individual identities and the multiple forms of translation needed to create dialogue between different aspects of their self-constructions and understanding of an issue. The role of the researcher in these types of reflective encounter is not to review a reconstruction of a 'paused' event, but to assist the participant in drawing out these fragmented elements and placing them within one form of dialogue or another.

How can researchers use video to focus participants' reflections?

In Chapter 2, we discussed the problems associated with showing videos to groups because of issues of selective attention and the nature of the visual memories of individuals. Using video within a reflexive modality increases these problems, as the researcher wants to direct, not only the attention of the participants, but also their reflections, towards specific aspects of the video. This, then, becomes even more problematic when we consider the range of reasons why participants might have not reflected on these areas in the first instance, from the complexity of any given interaction to it having the status of a taboo subject. In this section, we discuss a range of approaches through which researchers can use video to focus the attention of participants on areas that they have so normalised or routinised that they tend to ignore them; to get them to comment on issues that they feel it is tactless to mention; and to overcome the social and professional taboos that would normally silence them. These following examples involved practitioners from a range of services – education, youth and social work – involved in a variety of research projects, from relatively straightforward case studies to complex evaluations.

Stimulated recall in case studies of professional action (pause)

In this section, we discuss an amalgam of projects that meant that, for a period during the 1990s, we were consistently engaged in research projects in which we videoed professionals' practice and then used this to explore differing aspects of their knowledge base. We studied issues ranging from professionals' approaches to planning through to the frameworks they used to assess the work of others. To this day, we still use video to study practitioners, but now, because of the wider availability of the technology, we tend to do so in more participatory ways (see Chapter 5).

In our early projects, the process of focusing the reflections of participants would start as we built up a case study of their practice and began to highlight those areas they found difficult to describe. The video process would therefore be nested within a range of other data collection processes, the analysis of which began to highlight gaps and silences. The focus of the video would then be negotiated with the professional on the basis of the emergent findings from the case study. The video was treated as an additional data source within the case study and focused on gaps in our understanding. We initially tried reviewing videos using relatively unstructured stimulated recall protocols. In these reviews, participants would be given the opportunity to stop the video and discuss it whenever they were conscious of having changed their plans or found it difficult to make an assessment. Over the years, we have increased the degree of structure we impose on these reviews, partially because of the problems associated with waiting for a practitioner to stop the video as they gradually became more and more mesmerised by their appearance – it is not only students who need to habituate to the camera. The main issue, however, that led us to structure these debriefs was the difficulty participants faced in articulating their understandings, together with the complexity we faced in analysing them.

Relatively few researchers would now treat the recollections practitioners are prompted to make by video-based stimulated recall as accounts of their actual thinking at the time of the activity (Keith, 1988). In our own research, we have adopted an increasingly more phenomenological interpretation of what practitioners actually access when discussing what guides their actions or shapes their interpretations in complex professional contexts. Our changing approach arose from our habit of asking participants about the typicality of the sessions we were reviewing. We did this, initially, to allow us to make some assessment of the generalisability of the interpretations they were offering. We then began to notice that the responses generated by these questions could be related to general analytical frameworks used within various models of professional knowledge (Elbaz, 1983).

At first, we began to simply categorise their responses using three broad levels: rules of practice, practical principles and broad images that constituted the 'scripts' and sense-making frameworks that practitioners applied to complex situations. Rules are almost law-like aspects of these 'scripts' that describe highly structured responses and interpretations that they almost always engage in, or apply to, very specific interactions or situations. Practical principles are broader and indicate general 'tried and tested' approaches and interpretations that take into account a range of influences, from the moral to the contextual, that shape responses in a broad range of contexts. Finally, images range from an overarching 'ideal' image of how a particular process or activity should develop, to the more general rhythms, cycles, habits and rituals that shape practices. Fairly quickly, we began to use these levels as a

Table 3.1 Focusing differing forms of reflection

Roles of researcher and participants	The integration of video within the research process	Design and purpose of the video trigger	Strategies for processing the participants' reflections	Reasons for participants' lack of reflective awareness
Pause (Stimulated recall in case studies of professional action)				
The researcher creates a case study of the participant and within the limits of this they negotiate the focus of the video.	The video is only a small part of a number of different data sources within an overall case study.	An accurate recording of the event or activity under study. It can be based on a montage of examples or a single example.	Review video using 'Talk Aloud' or critical incidents during stimulated recall sessions.	Pressure and complexity of activities and contexts.
Translation (Video case studies of policy-making and implementation within public services)				
The researcher acts as a second-order action researcher supporting the practitioner to explore a current issue and their policy response to it.	Video is a means of the practitioner sharing their reconnaissance of an issue with colleagues. For the researcher it provides insights into how participants construct a policy issue.	Represents the construction of a social issue by practitioners, and their response to it in practice and is designed to be viewed with colleagues in order to gain their involvement.	Practitioners are engaged in a series of discussions with the researcher around the design of the video and its editing. Video is viewed collectively with colleagues.	Gradual accretion of insights, thoughts and beliefs over time.

means of structuring the actual video review sessions, rather than just analysing responses.

Within our later video feedback sessions, we explicitly compared and contrasted differing 'rules' and 'principles', and probed the relevance of a particular 'image'. We now consciously explore the anomalies and discontinuities of their application and their limitations. We treat these highly structured review video sessions as more akin to rational reconstructions (Habermas, 1972), aimed at making explicit consciously and unconsciously functioning rule systems, rather than attempts at broader self-reflection. Over time, we have come to restrict our aims for these review sessions, owing in part to the pragmatic pressures we find ourselves under which mean that we often do not have the opportunity to hold multiple review sessions with an individual practitioner. This shift is also a reflection of our increasing theoretical scepticism around what is actually stimulated by video recall and the ability of participants both to articulate their viewpoints and to manipulate them.

Video case studies of policy-making and implementation (translation)

If we are theoretical sceptics about the potential of video to stimulate the recollection of individuals about their activities within complex situations, what then is its potential to aid the far more complex reflective task of articulating and integrating much broader aspects of professional understandings? In our experience, if this involves simply viewing a video of practice, then very little. This is why, in part, we developed the idea of the trigger tape. Even with a really effective trigger tape, there is very little chance of achieving anything more than a general understanding of the status of an area or issue within the community or group being researched. By this, we mean the kinds of tension and contradiction it might throw up, or the degree of commonality of fragmentation in the response of participants to it. This is not to decry the potential of video or multimedia case studies in prompting reflection, or the potential of well-structured and facilitated professional development activities to support this level of reflection. It is simply that, within a reflective research modality that seeks new insights, we have found the most successful approach to using video is not as a medium to be watched by professionals but as a production process to engage them within.

The nature and degree of the participation of an individual within the video production process might vary considerably, depending upon the type of research methodology being employed and the resources available. In our own research, we have jointly developed videos with practitioners in projects ranging from evaluations to action research projects. To ensure that the video production process provides worthwhile and valid data collection opportunities, participants need to be given sufficient control over the process so that it reflects their areas of interest and concerns while being balanced with the areas of interest of the researcher. In the previous section, we characterised the process of focusing and structuring reflections of participants by watching a video 'trigger' as an act of rational reconstruction. Involving participants in the process of making a video around an issue is more akin to a reflective deconstruction of their understandings of it. They need to be encouraged to articulate and synthesise their fragmented understanding in order to ensure it is effectively represented on the final video product.

The project (Hadfield and Jardine, 1997) we want to use to exemplify our approach to treating video production as a means of supporting this type of reflection is one in which we acted as second-order action researchers (Elliott, 1991), supporting the work of a group of practitioners. These practitioners were enrolled in a Masters programme that looked at the development and implementation of public policies within urban contexts. IPSUP was run jointly between a university in England and another in the Netherlands. The programme had a strong comparative element based around joint visits and a number of satellite link-ups. During these link-ups, a series of video case studies, created by the course participants in both universities, were used to look at how, in different countries and cities, policy issues were constructed, and services were developed in response to them. The MA programme was designed to attract senior managers and leaders from a range of services, both public and voluntary. The cohorts of students in each university were supported by small teams of researchers and video consultants, who would assist them in making their video case studies.

There are a number of examples and models in the video literature (Schouten and Watling, 1997; Lunch and Lunch, 2006; Schouten, 2010) that demonstrate how to work with video 'novices' in a participatory way, but, in this case, we framed our video production process somewhat differently. First, we introduced it as part of a 'reconnaissance' of a policy area, the initial stage of a piece of action research, in which they would later make an intervention. Second, as this was to be a study of a policy issue, we introduced Ball's (1994) notion of policies being reconstructed at differing levels within a system as a means of moving them away from a simplistic, and often overly causal, distinction between policies being developed at one level of the system and then being delivered at another. In the video, they would be required to explore the reconstruction of a policy issue at different levels, from its inception at central and local government level to its reconstruction at the level of the city, their own service and 'on-the-ground' involvement of individual practitioners and service users. The theoretical notion of 'reconstruction' created a purpose and a rough structure for their video cases. Next, we asked them to look at these differing levels of the systems with a degree of equanimity, rather than either creating a hierarchy or using very different frames to explore each level. This was because we wanted them to treat the observations and insights of groups of service users with the same degree of criticality, and give them the same level of credence, as those of senior government policy-makers. Our first structuring device was therefore to take traditional macro-, meso- and micro-level approaches to policy analysis and then to separate out these levels and temporarily 'bracket' them so as to make them to some extent independent of each other. This was a first step in supporting the practitioners to deconstruct their narratives.

Traditional approaches to producing a video tend to operate with rough structures based around a timeline for the final product. This is then broken down into a series of smaller sections that represent the narrative chunking of the story that unfolds as the video plays. The danger in this form of rough structuring is that it can lead to overly cohesive and causal narratives, and we were interested in exploring the fragmented nature of individuals' understanding of the policy issue. We wanted to disrupt the causal narratives of the participants, which initially tended to move, in this instance, from policy development to policy implementation 'on the ground'. The next stage in the development of the reconnaissance was therefore to set about exploring the policy issues within these differing levels in a very specific way.

As senior managers, the participants were well versed in the language and politics of policy development. At some earlier stage in their careers, they had been front-line practitioners, but many had long since stepped back from day-to-day engagement with service users. Therefore, the first task we set them was aimed at reconnecting them with their earlier professional selves by getting them to explore the policy issue from the perspective of service users and front-line practitioners. We therefore asked them to start their filming at the level of front-line practice and service users. For example, a senior manager responsible for the support of young people spent evenings in a local youth club in their city, filming their perspectives on drug use, the microeconomics of drug dealing and their manipulation of the benefits system that surrounded them. These starting points were chosen as a means of reconnecting practitioners with aspects of their professional identities and understandings that they might not normally apply to a policy issue.

Once they had collected videos about each level of policy reconstruction, each was analysed separately using the same framework. This focused on identifying the tensions, dilemmas and paradoxes it appeared to present to those engaged in each level. In more simplistic terms, this was a search for points of connection and disconnection with their existing understandings of each level. The analysis was kept broadly thematic in order to facilitate their exploration of themes between levels. The next stage of analysis required them to consider if themes identified in one level were present in another, even if they did not appear to be directly related to the issue under consideration. This is where the flexibility of digital editing software would have been particularly useful, as it would have allowed us to juxtapose multiple small edits from different levels. At the time of the IPSUP project, we had to rely on crash editing tapes from cameras straight onto VCR. Many of the resulting juxtapositions of different parts of filming were fruitless and provided few insights into the understanding by participants of the situation, but many were connected in ways that were revealing and supported the participants to reflect on their own understandings. The juxtaposition of these different edits from their video and the discussions of the inferential processes that linked them in their minds becomes a physical enactment of the more metaphysical notion of placing differing 'small minds' into some form of dialogue. For example, one participant began to make connections between video that showed two young people describing how they organised the pooling of the last of their money with friends to purchase soft drugs, with video of two heads of service discussing tensions over trying to co-ordinate redundancies and a policy officer's account of multi-agency working. It prompted them to reflect on issues of collaboration and competition. They began to reflect, not just upon the formal policy of inter-service collaboration, but their personal theories as to why individuals do or do not collaborate, their own direct experiences of tensions and conflicts within partnership working, and the differences between interdependence and reciprocity. It was these thematic analyses that eventually provided the detailed structure of the final video products, the video case studies that would be shared with their colleagues.

The connections practitioners make between elements of the video materials at different points of the production process may or may not stand up to later scrutiny, and many will not influence the final edit of the video of the participant. What is important to the researcher is that they capture cycles of inferential connection-making and explore their relevance in practitioners' understanding of the issue. A final video product itself may or may not provide a useful analytical summary of an individual's understanding of an issue for the researcher, as audience effects often result in a product that is less concerned with revealing internal connections than with conveying an appropriate message. The videos produced as part of the IPSUP project reflected a number of such audience effects as they ranged along a continuum from relatively straightforward accounts of a policy issue to highly personal reflective accounts of participants' responses to a new policy discourse.

How do you design and use a video 'trigger tape' so that it supports participants to reflect?

In this last section, we want to provide a quick guide to constructing a trigger tape and then provide some hints as to how to use it effectively. Although there are various types of trigger, they share three key design stages:

- working the issue;
- deciding upon the key prompts;
- phasing the degree of challenge.

Working the issue

This takes us back to the idea that the trigger needs to connect with the different 'small minds' that exist within the individuals and the groups that are to be its audience. In this stage, the researcher needs to capture as many differing perspectives on an issue as possible, both from potential audiences and those who could be said to be stakeholders. Depending on how video is integrated into the research process, this may or may not require the collection of new data. What constitutes a 'different perspective' will also depend on whether some analysis has already been done on existing data, or if the production of a trigger is very early on in the research process. If the trigger is being created before any extensive analysis has been carried out, it might be a question of simply talking with individuals who are involved with the focal issue in differing ways. Towards the end of the production stage, as we feel we have collected sufficiently different viewpoints, we switch from considering whether the video illustrates a particular perspective to considering how well it represents this viewpoint. This might lead us to collecting additional material using techniques more akin to those of broadcast journalists than of researchers as we try and encapsulate a particular viewpoint as succinctly and powerfully as possible. We have to balance the significance of any issue with how well it is actually represented in the material we have recorded. This is counter to the tradition among most research approaches where analysis is superordinate to representation. In the process of building a trigger that is going to be an effective prompt, the situation is reversed. No matter how significant the issue is, and no matter how meaningful it may be to you as a researcher, if you are not able to capture an authentic representation of it during this phase, then it will not connect with the 'small minds' in the audience.

Deciding upon the key prompts

Once a range of different perspectives have been collected, rather than looking for themes that link them, we tend to carry out a form of 'cluster' analysis that identifies quotes and extracts that represent the differing types of 'small mind' we wish to connect among a potential audience. This type of analysis therefore operates at the boundaries between identifying culturally significant issues and representing them in ways in which they either embody a legitimate representation or challenge existing norms. This means clustering contrasting responses together and using their interplay as a means of highlighting different aspects of the issue and the variations in understanding the participants have of it. As we move towards the end of this stage, we are collecting together short segments of one or two minutes of video and starting to overlay contrasting voice-overs with differing images. By the end of this stage we have inevitably ended up with twice as many segments as can actually be used in the trigger video.

Phasing the degree of challenge

Once we have created more than enough segments to cover the range of interpretations we want to present, we set about selecting the most powerful and sequencing them into the final trigger tape. At this point, the overall design needs to take into consideration how the trigger will be shown to a potential audience. We tend to use triggers more frequently within focus groups than any other setting, and so we would now need to integrate it with the protocol we are developing for the focus group. We structure our focus groups around three to five sections, with each addressing a different aspect of the issue under consideration. The trigger tape is edited so that it introduces each section of the focus group and so it helps us maintain control in a relatively unobtrusive way. If the discussion starts to lose focus, unravel, become overly confrontational, run out of steam or be dominated by specific individuals, we can move on to a new section of the video.

The ideal length for any video stimulus is around three to five minutes, after which participants either switch into 'audience mode' and can become somewhat passive or become frustrated by the delay between their reaction to part of the video and having an opportunity to discuss it; this is particularly the case if they have reacted very negatively to the views being presented. The trigger video will therefore be broken down into sections lasting no more than five minutes. The sequencing of these sections is important and needs to mirror the general flow of a focus group. We therefore tend to begin with a section that introduces the overall focus and slowly progress to more and more specific, and potentially controversial, issues. This is done to help build a common understanding within the group concerning 'what we are about', and the relatively uncontroversial nature of the initial sections will hopefully encourage all its members to participate. Each section contains aspects that will be familiar and unfamiliar, but we gradually increase the level of challenge as the trigger tape progresses. We do this by increasing the number of conflicting statements and by increasingly focusing on more controversial viewpoints.

When we first started to use video in this way, the trigger tapes were literally that – tapes. This meant we tended to use them in a linear fashion, moving through each section from beginning to end. The only real flexibility we had was to fast-forward through a section if we felt it was not suitable at that time, or we wanted to link the previous discussion with a different section of the trigger tape. Now, with the increasing availability of DVD-editing software, we have the luxury of much more flexibility. We no longer have to work in such a linear fashion, as we can access different chapters of a DVD very easily during the focus group. This means we can make better links between sections of the trigger and the flow of discussion within the focus group. It also means that, by creating more chapters than we need, we can fine-tune the trigger tape to the group and pilot it as we use it. It is difficult to predict the nature of the reaction of a group to an issue, particularly if it is a sensitive area and we are showing it within a dynamic and unstable context. Piloting the trigger in a conventional way is therefore difficult and can be expensive, as drawing together a focus group is often time consuming and costly. The flexibility of the DVD allows us to fine-tune the trigger as we use it and be responsive to different groups' reactions.

In each type of reflective activity, pause and translation, video can play different roles. It can help pause the connections between thought and action and allow participants to reconstruct and examine their original interpretations. In terms of translation, video can bring together various aspects of an individual's fragmented understanding and put them into some form of dialogue. Watching a good trigger video can prompt both types of reflective activity, but for us the development of this idea was primarily a means of exploring theoretically and practically the different 'reflective' potential of participants in watching a video, compared with them producing a video, an issue we return to in Chapter 5.

Health Warning

Repeated showing of a video during stimulated recall can lead to participants showing the following symptoms:

➤ **False causality** – a general feeling of knowing what happened earlier on in a video because of having reviewed what occurred next. Participants tend to revise their views of the decisions and interpretations they made at the time, on the basis of knowledge they could not have had then.

Treatment – develop accounts of events before running forwards and backwards through them on the video.

➤ **Intensification** – participants tend to become over-concerned with an aspect of the interaction revealed on video that was relatively insignificant to them during the original interaction.

Treatment – distinguish between how they responded during the interaction as against what they are attending to on the video. Both are interesting sets of data, but do not mix while reviewing.

➤ **Rationality anxiety** – participants feel under pressure to produce rational accounts of why they did things in certain ways. This can result in them becoming anxious and defensive.

Treatment – reassure the participants that we are not always consciously aware of everything we do. We adopt routines and ways of working based on very implicit understandings.

Chapter 4

Video as projection and provocation

This chapter follows on from, and is an extension of, the previous chapter, concerning the use of video in a reflective mode. Our experience of working with video on a wide range of sensitive topics with hard-to-reach groups, and particularly young people, has led us to believe that video is particularly suited as means of disrupting the social and cultural mechanisms that ensure that certain areas are not 'naturally' foregrounded in everyday discussions within local communities or professional groups. Part of what defines one as a member of a group is the acceptance of its cultural norms and taboos, agreement on what constitutes an appropriate or worthwhile focus of discussion and action, and a willingness to submit to existing structures and hierarchies. To use video in a projective way is to create a form of stimulus that invites the audience to respond in ways that reveal to the researcher the social constructions that have been built up around 'taboo' subjects in communities, and reveals the extent and range of discourses surrounding these mythologies. Video in this modality is used as a way of unpacking issues through encouraging individuals to speak unguardedly in response to what they are seeing. An analysis of these 'unguarded responses' creates the space for the researcher to explore and gain a better understanding of how a phenomenon or set of issues is being constructed. Additionally, and powerfully, showing video as a social activity is a means of legitimating and 'kick-starting' discussions, particularly within tight-knit communities, that would not ordinarily be seen as appropriate, especially in the presence of an 'outsider'. The role of the researcher in this modality is to produce a video that provokes but allows for its audience to project onto its content, in a way that is distanced from them because it is not personal to them, and to create a temporary space in which participants can reveal a range of individual reactions which are normal, contradictory, paradoxical and 'normalised'.

The root metaphor

Video that moves continually between the provocative and more nuanced moments of projection is best thought of as being an act of temporary social re-attunement. In providing moments that both provoke and calm, the aim of the video is to provide the space in which individuals feel safe to play around with social norms in a way that they would not normally do. For these reasons, we have found it difficult to think of one metaphor that encompasses this continual movement. It is easier to think of the acts of projection and provocation separately, and so we have variously thought of metaphors from the Rochard test, in which an individual is presented with unambiguous images and asked to create meaning from them, to the metaphor of the big screen event. Setting up a big screen in a pub for people to watch a big sporting event does involve legitimating a temporary change of space from being in a location in which people might eat a meal or have a quiet drink to one where the audience can shout, chant, swear at the game or abuse individual players, teams or match officials. This is a somewhat unsatisfactory metaphor, in that the images the audience are watching are mostly unambiguous – after all, it is in the round the 'game' they are watching

– but there always seem to be plenty of provocative moments often focusing around disputed tackles or interpretations of the rules. On the other hand, it does capture the dynamism of the temporary space, if not necessarily the more nuanced idea of provocation and projection as acts of re-attunement.

To recap, a video trigger aimed at re-attuning individuals' reflective gaze needs to create a space in which, at least temporarily, it is legitimate to challenge assumptions and norms and to discuss these in ways that would normally be seen as unacceptable. Therefore, when we develop a video stimulus to re-attune the reflective gaze of participants we design it as a 'projective' activity, a different design specification from that of a 'reflective' trigger tape. This is because, in research terms, the utility of reflective tasks and processes is that they promote participants to introspect, that is, look inwards on their own conceptions and motivations, and then articulate these in ways that are meaningful to the researcher. Paradoxically, the major limita-tion of such reflective tasks is a mirror of their strengths, in that participants can become overly conscious of what they are revealing to the researcher, and this can lead them to engage in self-censorship and consciously manipulate what they discuss with the researcher. The central paradox is that increased self-reflection, resulting in greater self-awareness, may well moderate participants' willingness to discuss a taboo area or confront a particular social norm. As they become more conscious of the issue by focusing on it, they also become aware of the mechanisms and sanctions that operate to keep it in the corner of their reflective gaze. They might not wish to expose themselves, or others, to the disapproval and sanctions that might result from dragging such an issue centre stage.

Projective tasks and processes invert the reflective process, in that they are ostensibly about commenting upon the views of others, and not about participants revealing their own views. They are particularly useful in areas where there is a cacophony of voices but no dialogue, because different voices slide past each other. A projective task aims to get participants to project their own views and understandings onto the video stimulus presented to them. The trigger video is therefore designed to encourage then to articulate their initial, and to a degree unreflective, reactions to others' actions and interpretations. Once these have been articulated and accepted by the group watching the video as a commentary on what has been presented to them, rather than as revealing the viewpoint of an individual, it becomes much easier to explore and critically challenge them. Viewing a projective trigger video creates a space in which it is acceptable to discuss the unacceptable, or the ignored, because what apparently are being discussed are not the views of individuals taking part in the discussion, but those represented on the video. It is those on the video who have broken the 'rules' and deserve to be sanctioned; meanwhile, those in the 'audience' have a degree of permission to discuss why this is the case, and collectively reflect on how these views have come about and the influences that have shaped them, without being construed as necessarily challenging or threatening these norms. As long as the focus of the discussion remains upon the views represented in the video, then participants can challenge accepted norms, discuss their limitations and present alternatives, with little fear of being sanctioned, as they are simply responding to 'what was on the tape'.

Issues of exposure and sanctions were something we had to consider long and hard when we were exploring young people's constructions of risk and how their 'risk repertoire' (Haw, 2006a, 2009a, 2010b) changed, in response to the context and social group they were within. Depending on whether they were with their families or peer groups, or if the interactions being studied took place within schools or local communities, they engaged in very different patterns of risk-taking and constructed what was a 'risk' differently. Here, the fragmented nature of their social identities as 'risk-takers' was theorised as arising from the somewhat contradictory norms they faced, and had to mediate, as they moved in and out of a range of groups, institutions and communities. In this project, participants' levels of self-awareness of their fragmented identities varied, resulting in some being able to articulate the contradictory nature of their actions and understandings, whereas others failed to recognise their shifts and inconsistencies. In this project, we used a 'trigger' video at the beginning of the research, and its use in a project aimed at articulating young people's views on risk taking is discussed more fully in Chapter 6.

A projective trigger tape needs to present a range of perspectives, from those that are apparently supportive of the taken-for-granted assumptions of the viewing group, to others that directly challenge accepted norms. This is key to encouraging group members to reflect on the norms whose acceptance binds them together. Within tight-knit groups and local communities, it is often difficult to get members to express these counter-cultural views. One strategy we have used is to edit together images with contrasting voice-overs in order to highlight contradictions between espoused values and norms and the practices or 'realities' of a situation. The more extreme the contrasting views contained within the trigger, the more likely that individuals will project their own interpretations on to them. Some will do this in order to bolster the legitimacy of the 'acceptable', whereas others will offer support to the challenge presented by the counter-culture. There is a point at which the alternative or critical views expressed within the video can lose their ability to prompt a response. This occurs when such views are taken by the group to be so extreme that they can dismiss them as unrepresentative or unrelated to their own work. A degree of craft and insight into the group under study is required by the researcher to create a video trigger that treads this line between getting individuals to project their own understandings onto a video and dismissing it as irrelevant.

To set out the practical implications of these notions of attunement and re-attunement and the use of video in the processes of projection and provocation, we want to discuss two projects. The first is a piece of work we did in prisons with prisoners and prison officers about their perceptions of full body searching, and the second is a piece of inter-generational work recently carried out in a specific Muslim community that originated from the Azad Kashmir region of Pakistan. The trigger video we made for the first project was much more about attunement, as we reconstructed a 'by-the-book' full body search, whereas the final DVD made for the second project had a greater emphasis on re-attunement, because its aim was to provoke a dialogue among those outside this community by challenging their existing views of this group.

Video reconstructions of full body searches (attunement)

The process of attunement is based on redirecting individuals' reflective gaze. How then might video be used to help people reflect upon areas that are culturally taboo? In any community, social or professional, conventions exist about what is an appropriate focus of conversation and what is morally attended to. Social norms embodied in tacit rules decree what is noticed or ignored, what is relevant or irrelevant, and so community members are socialised into framing only certain parts or aspects of their situations, while systematically ignoring others. If the rules and sanctions are sufficiently strong, then these aspects can become taboos, and members of a community who draw attention to them or discuss them will be treated as social deviants. These taboos can vary in strength, from the general approbation that surrounds the belief that one 'should not wash one's dirty linen in public', to the exertion of considerable power and influence to sustain certain conspiracies of silence, such as institutional racism or domestic violence.

In this section, we consider how, in one project, we attempted to use a trigger video to broach a strong social taboo, discussion of the process of full body searching, colloquially termed 'strip searching', among prisoners and prison officers. The project was an exploration of the experiences and attitudes of prisoners and prison officers across seven prisons in England. Full body searches are a taboo subject in such communities, for a number of reasons. First, they are moments of extreme vulnerability for prisoners, in which they can feel at their most exposed to the influence that prison officers have over them. Second, among prison officers, they are potential points of conflict at which prisoners may object to being searched and in which they themselves may be accused of unprofessional behaviour. They can also be very intimate and visceral moments, in which prison officers have to deal with a range of prisoners, from those with a lack of personal hygiene to those who might previously have been physically or sexually abused. Finally, in the 'macho' culture within male prisons, where prisoners use homophobic banter as a form of defence mechanism or as resistance towards officers, discussing any type of vulnerability might quickly be classified as 'deviant'. What these taboos have resulted in is a general normalisation of the full body search procedure, something that is generally accepted as part of the prison routine, an irrelevance in comparison with the quality of the food, contact with visitors and the quality of the library service.

Early on in the research, it became clear that we would have only relatively limited access to both prisoners and prison officers, and the main form of data collection would have to be a questionnaire survey, supplemented by a number of focus groups, as the funders wanted a comprehensive review. We therefore set out to develop a trigger video that could be used in a range of contexts, both mediated by ourselves, when used with focus groups, and as a stand-alone prompt, when shown to those completing the questionnaire. How, then, to draw this taboo area back into focus and do so in a way that would stop its discussion becoming stereotypical, as individuals rushed to adopt the security of the traditional positions on offer to them?

Our research started with a series of interviews with prisoners and prison officers across several prisons in England, including male and female establishments. These focused on their experiences and perceptions of full body searches, and they were all recorded. We also visited a training centre for prison officers, where we had the opportunity to see aspects of their training and to talk with some of the trainers who worked with new staff. The overall design of the trigger video arose out of our analysis of these interviews and the fact that we only had sufficient funding to create two trigger tapes, one for use in male establishments, the other female, and therefore each would have to be suitable for use with prisoners and prison officers. The analysis revealed a number of issues that, in differing forms, affected both officers and prisoners. Key was the theme of what constituted a correct or appropriate way of carrying out a search. Perhaps somewhat surprisingly, considering the detail in the training manual, prison officers revealed in private that they were concerned over whether they were still 'doing it right' – they knew that practices varied slightly between prisons;

and they were anxious about searching certain categories of prisoners who, for religious reasons, might object to being searched. Prisoners, on the other hand, were more likely to talk about whether they could be asked to do certain things during a search, what should happen to their clothes, and the appropriateness of the banter engaged in by officers. What was also striking was that both groups talked about the embarrassment and humiliation inherent in the process and their shared dislike of the situation.

Taken together, these overlapping concerns provided us with a starting point for the design. We decided to base the trigger around a reconstruction of a strip search, but one that would present it being done exactly 'by the book', including using diagrams from the official manual. The idea was that it would represent a challenge to both groups' accepted views of how the procedure was carried out in practice, but would be legitimated by its use of official literature. We believed that this would be an ideal projective image, as it could not be rejected as completely unrealistic but, in its 'pristine state', was sufficiently different from each group's experience to promote a range of reactions, not least of which was why it was an unrealistic representation. Around the central conceit of the reconstruction, we wrapped various extracts from the interviews. These were carefully chosen so that it was initially difficult to identify whether the speaker was a prisoner or prison officer. The quotes presented a range of counter-cultural observations, so that, for example, prison officers could be heard discussing the humiliation inherent in the process or querying its effectiveness. These were edited against prisoners discussing its role in keeping them safe and how some officers carried it out in ways that maintained their dignity. The reconstruction itself was broken down into three sections, at the end of which questions were posed to the audience. These sections were carefully sequenced so that they moved from more technical questions about the nature of the procedure to increasingly more critical questions that questioned its status and application as a security procedure. This sequencing was seen as crucial in moving on their discussions of a taboo from the actuality of the procedure to questioning its status within their 'community'. This represented an increasing level of challenge for those who carried out the procedure and those who were its target.

The focus groups were not mixed and so consisted of either prisoners or prison officers. Their responses to the trigger tape were revealing in terms of what makes an effective trigger. All of the focus groups, to differing degrees, reacted to the 'idealised' version of the search procedure represented in the video. If this created a space in which participants felt able to discuss the differences between their realities and what was presented to them in the video, what tipped them into the most critical discussions were the voice-overs. What affected the focus group members most acutely was that they were unable, at times, to distinguish between prisoners' and prison officers' comments. At times, this could be used by the researchers to challenge the assumptions made by focus group members and so start to break down certain stereotypical assumptions about how prisoners and prison officers felt about the procedure. Although these challenges were useful in challenging assumptions that each group felt about the other, they were more powerful in challenging within group norms. The gradual progression of the trigger video also allowed the discussions to move on from 'technical' disputes over what may or may not occur within the procedure to much more fundamental reassessments of its worth as a security measure.

The construction of an effective trigger, capable of promoting reflection around a 'taboo' issue, requires an in-depth understanding not only of the issue but also what gives it a taboo status. It needs to create a space that allows the topic to be discussed by enabling participants to project their own perceptions and experiences onto it. These periods of projection need to be followed up by critical discussions of the norms expressed within them. To an extent, these challenges can be embedded within the trigger tape, but the researcher will still need to follow them through. The strength of embedding these within the trigger is the legitimacy given to such challenges when they are articulated by in-group members rather than by a researcher. In the following section, we will return to the issue of designing an effective trigger tape.

The construction of the being, becoming, belonging DVD: re-attunement

To end this chapter, we consider a research project that invited members of a particular Muslim community to participate in making a video that was, in part, conceived of as an act of resistance to how they are being stereotypically set up and positioned by others. Through a process of re-attunement, the aim was to produce a film that would provoke those outside Muslim communities to rethink how they view Muslims, while at the same time reflecting on how they themselves are being positioned within their own social norms and discourses, predominantly through information, gleaned from the media, that encourages them to view these communities in particular ways. The difference here was that we were making a DVD, not at the beginning of a project to broach a strong taboo such as full body searching, but at the end of a project that, by representing findings that were not obviously in the public psyche, could stimulate a process of re-attunement and, therefore, a more reflexive dialogue.

The purpose of the research was to study the shifting identities of British Muslims by returning to the same participants and their families who had taken part in a piece of doctoral research carried out over a decade ago. The research explored how the women who had taken part in the original research while still schoolchildren had since constructed their identities now they were adults, many with their own children, and in employment. The original work was carried out in a single-sex state school with a high proportion of Muslim girls and a private Muslim girls' school (Haw, 1995, 1998) and it set out to understand the roles played by these schools in socialising pupils into British society by exploring the debates around how excluded groups are drawn into democratic life and the key tensions arising from notions of inclusion and exclusion.

The more recent research, carried out between 2008 and 2010, revisited some of the original participants and their families, with the help of two co-researchers whose families took part in the original research. The aim of this research was to:

- reveal the shifts and changes that have occurred over the intervening years between both pieces of work; and
- explore the 'everdayness' of Muslim families in contemporary Britain.

The original research was carried out against the backdrop of the Gulf War, the Salman Rushdie affair and an ensuing debate within the British media concerning the extent to which these communities should, or could, be assimilated into British society. The recent research was carried out in the period post 9/11 and 7/7, in a period where wider social 'myths' to do with, for example, Muslim women as the 'oppressed other', the 'mothers of home-grown terrorists' and 'my son the fanatic', are widely circulated through a range of media, from the newspapers to the Fitna video on YouTube, and from dramatic representations in soap operas to the work of intelligence agencies. It was also carried out at a time when individuals were increasingly recognised as active consumers and producers of culture.

Data were generated in two ways: first, through the research team working with participants and their families to make video diaries that filmed aspects of everyday lives and reflected the narratives of different generations within the same families, of life in Britain and how this has changed. Second, we carried out a series of individual and group interviews focused around the three themes, educational and school experiences, notions of identity and citizen-ship, and notions of religious identity. The purpose of these was twofold: first, to provide an additional layer of data that could be analysed to provide themes around which we could analyse shifting aspects of identities and explore changes in attitudes to living in modern, multicultural Britain; and, second, to be used as voice-overs when we made the DVD at the end of the project.

We also hosted a school reunion that we videoed and recorded, and attended different community and school events, such as multicultural evenings, end-of-term concerts and social events. Some of these interviews used a trigger video made for the European Year Against Racism (Hadfield and Haw, 2000a), newspaper articles and photographs as prompts. An analysis of the video diaries, the interviews and these different events revealed a complex story.

The participants form part of an 'in-between generation' that visibly marks a moment within British multicultural society in terms of being British, being Muslim and being British Muslims (Haw, 2009b, 2010a). They are an in-between generation in the sense that their identity is, in part, defined by their active reconstruction and re-evaluation of the relationship between the traditions they inherited from their parents and the role of religion within them, and the relationship of those traditions and religious beliefs with British culture and identity. The short time between both pieces of research has been a time of major changes within their communities in terms of a broadening of attitudes to education, work, marriage and the role of women, in part as a reflection of the broader changes in British society. As young people, they were provided with a strong sense of British identity via their parents' moral discourses: a notion of Britishness often based on espoused ideals of tolerance and fairness. Prepared by their parents to live within this idealised society and educate their children in its values, as parents themselves they have instead been presented with the rise of the 'lad and ladette' culture. Their felt contradictions between contemporary and traditional moral views of Britishness have been played out against a backdrop of a globalised youth and media culture. They have been faced with an emergent British identity, now less based on their parents' traditional notions of tolerance and fairness, and rather increasingly based on normalising difference (what it is to be British) and problematising the 'difficult' (increasing intolerance of that which is seen as non-British).

They also are part of a generation that is in the process of reconstructing and reintegrating both their parents' traditional and cultural notions of being Muslim and their idealisation of British identity. This has led to the partial rejection of some traditional values, running in parallel with the reassertion of other religious values. As a result, they have become 'more confident to be seen as Muslim', but are often in a dialogue with their own children and parents as to what constitutes being Muslim in Britain, partly because of events such as 9/11 and 7/7. As these communities have gained confidence in living, working and actively participating in a British multicultural society, they have experienced an intense mixture of increased personal confidence in being Muslim, with a heightened social sense of how Muslims are constructed in the media and their own communities. In part, these young women are members of communities that are being socially constructed as becoming 'more Muslim', and this has further intensified their reflections on their identity and how prevalent social constructions impact upon them and their families. Many are now part of communities that are beginning to draw back into themselves in response to living in a society where fear of 'the other' is widespread.

The challenge when making the video was to make something that would reflect these outward changes, while also reflecting the changes that had happened within their communities as they were growing up, and the complexities, contradictions and paradoxes that were part of their everyday lives as they considered what it means to be legally seen as British citizens but socially constructed and often treated as other than British. Overlapping the findings of the research with these concerns provided us with a starting point for the design. Additionally, previous experience of using video as a way of re-attuning audiences through the processes of projection and provocation has led us to a realisation that the film has to be short and in 'bite-sized' pieces. This meant producing a video that was not more than fifteen minutes long in its entirety and that was made in short sections.

In the end, and after much discussion, we decided on three sections. We wanted the video to be in a similar format to the Urbanfields project discussed in Chapter 5, with titles picking out key words from the voice-overs and with each section posing a key question or giving a focus for discussion at the end, like the full body searching DVD. A starting point for us was to 'name' the three sections. The first section we called 'Being British', the second 'Being Muslims' and the third 'Becoming British Muslims?' In this way, we thought we could get over the idea of linear transitions over time, in this case twenty years, and inward changes and transitions, both within the community and external to it. Our next challenge was to make decisions about the overall feel for each section. To try and get over the notion of linear time, we decided that the first section should have the feel of a 1950s/1960s Britain, which is when many of these families first immigrated to Britain. To convey a sense of rapid change within these communities, we decided on a section that had a nostalgic feel to it, one that looked back on an idealised past. The second section had to have the feel of 'in-betweenness' and transition, while setting the scene for a more 'edgy' third section that questioned the idea of being British Muslims in a time when media-driven discourses have come to dominate. Like the full body searching DVD, but in a different way because this was an end product, the sections were therefore carefully sequenced so that they moved from a more narrative structure about what it means to be British to ask increasingly more critical questions of its audience about what that means to those who are born here but separated from the mainstream for a variety of reasons. This sequencing was seen as crucial to providing a temporary safe space for its audiences to move between unguarded reaction to a reaction that has the potential to prompt more positive dialogue, as they move from stereotypical discussions of, for example, terrorism and the oppression of women, to considerations of the actuality of the everyday and questioning the status of these dominant and often media-driven discourses within their 'community'.

Given these considerations, the first section starts gently by taking its audience down memory lane and, against quintessential British scenes and symbolic representations, such as the 'British bobby', the Queen, a traditional roast dinner, there were voice-overs in a range of accents, from those born in Scotland to the North, Midlands and Southern regions, reminiscing about family Sunday dinners and primary school days. It is not until the end of the section that a caption reveals the names of the people the audience have been listening to and that these are obviously Muslim names and the individuals were either born here or came here at a very early age.

Having provoked the audience to make some 'unguarded' assumptions, the aim of the next two sections was to provide a series of images and voice-overs onto which the audience could project. It had to give them a representation of issues and events that had been already processed, creating a safe place for collective reflection because it was part of common parlance. In a piece of research dealing with difficult and sensitive issues, where there was a great deal of tension around what could be talked about and what could not, the section needed to provide the space to discuss and 'play' with these wider issues by providing the sort of content that 'lived' sufficiently within the experiences of the audience, so that there was an existing awareness while being ambiguous enough for individuals to realise that they had hold of different understandings of them. The section begins with a picture of a young Muslim woman wearing the hijab, which is the Union Jack. The footage in this section is mainly taken from the video diaries, school reunion and social and community events. The voice-overs are a selection of quotes that juxtapose what they believed their parents wanted for them and their own experiences as they grew up, from trying to 'blend in' and reflecting on their susceptibility to conform to cultural trends such as punk and grunge, to making decisions to start wearing the hijab and visibly mark their difference. The section ends with an individual asking such questions as, 'What constitutes "Britishness"?' and 'When do you truly become British?' and, from there, reflecting on 'When do you stop being abused about going home?' and, therefore, 'Where is home?'

The last section deliberately 'ups the ante'. It was purposively story-boarded. It incorporates a series of stills, such as newspaper articles that are overtly Islamophobic, and is filmed against the backdrop of a beamed, eighteenth-century cottage over an evening that features two Muslim women watching television, eating and surfing online dating sites, to get across to the audience a developing sense of their agency and the choices they are having to make about living in contemporary British multicultural society, post 9/11 and 7/7. The voice-overs are deliberately provocative, and some were chosen because they directly place blame on the role of the media. They were also chosen to reveal their reflections about what being Muslim means and an emerging questioning of the British part of their identities. We include the following voice-over here because it so accurately sums up these complexities:

> I think particularly youth and young people nowadays, if you give young people a label which if you put on the television Muslims are given a label aren't they? I think today's generation rather than putting their head in the sand and kind of denying who they are I think they'd actually stick their heads out of the sand and say yes we are Muslim and we're very proud. I don't think, what I am trying to say is people don't aspire to the negative image that we are given by the media of Muslims being terrorists or women being oppressed women, in fact I think a lot of young Muslim people are very confidently saying actually I am a Muslim woman and I feel very proud of wearing the hijab, very proud of wearing the habiyah but I am not oppressed. I can actually speak for myself and speak very confidently and I'm, you know, I will tell you about Islam. And I think similarly for say yes we're Muslim and we're very proud and you, they'll be able to talk about, you know, international politics and they'll also be able to say and we are not bloody terrorists either.

The intended audience for this video is somewhat eclectic, ranging from young people in more formal and informal education settings tied into citizenship programmes, to CPD training with professionals and practitioners. Each section is designed to stand alone, so that discussion can follow, or the video can be viewed in its entirety. We have learned from producing similar videos, such as Urbanfields and the full body search reconstruction, that it is best to keep the video as simple and as short as possible. The reasons for this are to do with stimulus overload diverting attention from the main issues for discussion, but are more importantly to do with methodological dilemmas around mediating its viewing. The construction of an effective trigger capable of promoting reflection around a 'taboo' issue requires an in-depth understanding, not only of the issue, but also of what gives it a taboo status. It needs to create a space that allows the topic to be discussed by enabling participants to project their own perceptions and experiences onto it. These periods of projection need to be followed up by critical discussions of the norms expressed within them. To an extent, these challenges were embedded within the trigger tape designed to provoke and project discussions about full body searching, but the researchers who designed the video were there to follow them through. This is not the case when the video is the end product of a process, rather than a product that front-ends a piece of research. The challenge here of embedding complex and sensitive issues within the trigger is the legitimacy given to such challenges when they are articulated by in-group members and are put together in such a way that they can stand alone and be mediated by others. Relinquishing control over its viewing does, we would argue, present the researcher with a very different and somewhat more complex set of methodological and ethical challenges, which are further discussed in the last chapters of the book.

DANGER

HEAVY

MACHINERY

DO NOT USE A TRIGGER TAPE TO DO ALL THE 'HEAVY LIFTING'.

A TRIGGER TAPE ON ITS OWN CANNOT GUIDE PARTICIPANTS THROUGH SOPHISTICATED ACTS OF PROJECTION.

PLEASE ENSURE IT IS USED BY AN EXPERIENCED OPERATOR.

KEEP THE TRIGGER SIMPLE, SHORT AND TARGET THE KEY ISSUES.

Chapter 5

Video that generates participation

In exploring the role of video in generating participation, we want primarily to focus on three key stages in the participatory research process: the use of video as an invitation in the recruitment/access/entry process; the use of video as an icebreaker in the negotiation of research foci; and its use to help understand and manage a range of relationships. Other stages, to do with the representation of different voices in the video and its design and dissemination, will be alluded to, because they are closely linked to, and dependent on, the others, but they are more fully discussed in the following chapter on video and the articulation of voice.

To start unpacking the potential and limitations of using video in this modality, we need to consider two key issues. First, in what kinds of participatory research video has been used, and, second, how these projects have integrated video to perform different roles in the research process. In considering the first question, we will use examples from a range of work, but, for the second question, we refer to two of our own research projects. The first is a project, Urbanfields, carried out as part of an ESRC priority network, 'Pathways into and out of crime: risk, resilience and diversity'. It was concerned to explore how young people constructed their notions of risk. In this project, we needed to pay attention to how young people's 'risk repertoire' (Farrington and Loeber, 1998; Farrington, 2000) changed depending upon:

- the context and social group they were within;
- whether they were with their families or peer groups;
- if the interactions being studied took place within schools or local communities.

In this project, the fragmented nature of their social identities as 'risk takers' was theorised as arising from the somewhat contradictory norms they faced, and had to mediate, as they moved in and out of a range of groups, institutions and communities. Their level of self-awareness of their fragmented identities also varied, resulting in some being able to articulate the contradictory nature of their actions and understandings, whereas others failed to recognise their shifts and inconsistencies.

We regard this project as an example of our most sophisticated work with video, simply because it is one of our more recent projects, and we were able to build on all our previous experiences of using video in different modalities. This project spanned modalities, and so we refer to it as being multimodal. Its multimodal nature arises from, first, the making of a trigger tape designed to translate and attune young people to notions of risk (see Chapters 3 and 4), and to recruit and gain access and entry to groups of young people; and, second, the fact that we used it to generate multiple layers of young people's understanding of their everyday lives as they made their own films. In this phase of the work, it was about bringing their agendas to the fore. These agendas were not necessarily ours, nor ones we agreed with, but, by filming and recording the young people as they made, discussed and viewed their own videos, we were able to make our own stand-alone product at the end of the project (Haw, 2006b). This more mediated product was designed to challenge the views of practitioners and the dominant discourses in the criminal justice system, where the notion of risk factors is being used to predict offending behaviour and as a justification for early intervention strategies. By interleaving the discussions of young people, with some of their footage, as well as our own filming, with voice-overs from young people and professionals, and using professional editors, we were able to juxtapose audio and video as a way of provoking discussion.

The second project we want to refer to was funded by the Joseph Rowntree Foundation, as part of an initiative aimed at raising the voice of young people in preventive work with families. This project involved a team of university researchers working in partnership with community youth workers, a group of young men who had been, or were at risk of being, excluded from school, and their school. We worked together mainly at a local house, used by community youth workers as a drop-in centre. The house was part of a larger programme concerned with young people and their drug usage. We met every Wednesday morning to help the young men make a video about their experiences of being excluded from school, and we facilitated the showing of their film to audiences of their choice, which included staff and governors.

The root metaphor

Our root metaphor for thinking about video in participatory research is the metaphor of the 'good party'. In this metaphor, the researcher is the host, the party is the participatory project and the video is the entertainment. A good party is one that can be enjoyed by everybody, even though they arrive with different expectations and needs, and one in which everyone contributes to the entertainment. At a party, the host has the initial responsibility for bringing it all together and creating the context for everyone else to enjoy themselves. But, once things really get going, it becomes the guests' party, and to make it work they have to put effort and enthusiasm into it. In the end, they are in charge of the entertainment, and they need to think of the enjoyment of others and take responsibility for what happens.

At the parties we run, the guests usually don't know each other well. They consist of little cliques, and some might not even know us directly, as they have been dragged along by someone we have invited. During the party, people will come and go, some will arrive early and never leave, whereas others will turn up late and bring life back to a flagging event.

A good host needs to put on differing types of entertainment at different points of the party, whether it be some food to bring people together, some music to get people dancing or just a place for people to chill out. In the end, a successful party is one in which people find the greatest entertainment and enjoyment from being with the other guests. The good host works hard to achieve this by looking out for the needs of individual guests, bringing people together who might be interested in each other, and diplomatically dealing with any trouble. For us, the party is a powerful root metaphor for thinking about the use of video to generate participation. The start of a party might require some formal entertainment, to provide an initial reason for people coming together and to help them feel comfortable, and a good trigger video can have a role here. In the end, it is the interaction between the guests that makes the party, and so it is how the participants engage with each other, the researcher and those they film during the video process that makes for an effective participatory project.

The preliminary stage of organising a party involves decisions about who to invite and what sort of party it is going to be. At this stage, a trigger video can play the role of an invitation and advertise the event. The guests will be those who are interested in making a video, and they will turn up with some ideas and expectations about what this means to them, what sort of video is going to be made and what it is going to be about. Once the party starts, there are many different relationships to manage. The views of people have to be listened to and taken into consideration. At this point, the hosts can use a 'here's one I made earlier' video as an icebreaker, to get the party going and to get some understanding of the interests of the guests and their abilities with regard to the technical and creative aspects of the video process. Hosting a good party requires a certain amount of preparation and the sensitivity to see when to retreat into the background or maintain a high profile. This is often dependent on the personality of the hosts and their notions of what being a host means to them. Once the party has finished, there are the inevitable reflections about what went well and what was less successful.

What kinds of participatory research has video been used in?

Participatory research has a long history, and its growing popularity inevitably means that the debates about the issues it raises are both contested and complex. We want to begin this section with a brief overview that illustrates its proliferation and, through identifying the commonalities that run across different approaches, highlights why video has become a popular tool in participatory research. It is claimed that participatory research is an alternative philosophy of social research, because it makes a commitment to be responsive to the needs of 'ordinary people' and makes no claim to neutrality or to serving the needs of the wealthy and the powerful (Park *et al.*, 1993; McTaggart, 1997). The role of 'ordinary people' throughout the process can take different forms, from those who are trained and supported to become researchers themselves, to those who work as co-researchers and have an equality of input to the whole design process, to those who are little more than engaged participants. Participatory research is often defined as systematic inquiry, with the collaboration of those affected by the issue being studied, for the purposes of education and taking action or effecting change. It has three key elements: people, power and praxis (Finn, 1994). It is people-centred in the sense that the process of critical inquiry is informed by, and responds to, the experiences and needs of the people involved. In participatory research, a project is not just carried out to generate 'facts', but to develop understanding of the self and context of the self. It is about understanding how to research, allowing people to become self-sufficient learners and to evaluate knowledge that others generate. Good participatory research helps develop relationships of solidarity by bringing people together to collectively research, study, learn and then act. There is no off-the-shelf formula, step-by-step method or 'correct' way to do participatory research. Rather, participatory methodology is best described as a set of principles and a process of engagement in the inquiry.

This emphasis on reflection and change in participatory research means that it has much in common with action research, and, unsurprisingly, given the predilection of academics to define and label as a means of claiming uniqueness and difference, one trajectory of the approach has become known as participatory action research (PAR). Kemmis and McTaggart (2000) note seven features of participatory action research. It is:

- a social process;
- participatory, engaging people in examining their knowledge;
- practical and collaborative;
- emanicipatory;
- critical;
- recursive (reflexive, dialectical).

Arguably, the feature that sets PAR apart from other forms of participatory research is this emphasis on change within the process. Participatory action research is rooted in Freire's notion of 'challenging the habit of submission' and overcoming the frame of mind that curtails people from fully and critically engaging with their world and civic life (Freire, 1978). It is a democratic process, where researchers and participants are actors, influencing the flow, interpreting the content and sharing options for action. Ideally, this collaborative process is empowering because it:

- brings isolated people together around common problems and needs;
- validates their experiences as the foundation for understanding and critical reflection;
- presents the knowledge and experiences of the researchers as additional information upon which to reflect critically;
- contextualises what have previously felt like 'personal', individual problems or weakness;
- links such personal experiences to political realities.

In a similar vein, community-based participatory research (CBPR) is conducted as an equal partnership between traditionally trained 'experts' and members of a community, often self-defined. The difference, perhaps, is its emphasis on collaboration between 'formally trained research' partners from any area of expertise, provided that what the researcher supplies is deemed to be useful to the investigation, fully committed to a partnership of equals and the production of a piece of work that has usable outcomes. Like its other branches, CBPR is an iterative process, incorporating research, reflection and action in a cyclical process.

Although some individuals find the nuances of these definitions helpful, others do not, but they do serve to identify the common threads that explain why video has become such a popular tool in these approaches. Basically, if you are involved in an investigation and an analysis of a problem with a group of people whose lives are directly affected by that problem, then your research can be described as participatory. Ideally, your investigation will lead to action. Finally, participatory research differs from the more conventional kind done by experts, usually identified with academics such as ourselves, in that it does not take decision-making away from the 'ordinary' people. Instead of becoming dependent on experts, participants become experts themselves. Equitable partnerships require the sharing of power, resources, credit, results and knowledge, as well as a reciprocal appreciation of each partner's knowledge and skills at each stage of the project, including problem definition/ issue selection, research design, conducting research, interpreting the results and determining how the results should be used for action. These core characteristics necessarily affect how you, as researchers, conduct yourself in the research context and how you manage a range of different relationships.

For this type of approach to be successful, the onus is on you to take a certain number of risks and be flexible, and this is not always easy when you have deadlines to meet and funders to please. Projects undertaken under the banner of these different types of participatory research can loosely be grouped as:

- community consultations;
- end users–service users engagement;
- advocacy projects;
- NGO education programmes, run alongside or within broader research activities.

However you decide to label your research or place it in any of the above groups, the need to develop the participation of 'ordinary people' in research, whatever their role, creates key methodological challenges to do with the representation of different epistemological standpoints, voice and issues of equity, power and dynamic models of identity. In terms of the party metaphor, every project you develop will involve you in a number of decisions before, during and after the project. As a host are you going to:

- keep a high profile and presence throughout the party;
- let others take charge of certain aspects of it, effectively working with a team that brings different types of expertise for doing the music, providing food or meeting and greeting;
- stay very much in the background, facilitating when things seem to lose momentum, constantly reidentifying and engaging those needed to keep the party going;
- act as a back-up when others begin to flag;
- act as matchmaker, putting people in contact who previously didn't know each other;
- be the one to deal with the aftermath, organising the clearing up when it has finished and running interference with those on the outside of the event (gate crashers).

Given this emphasis on 'ordinary people', praxis and power, it is hardly surprising that video has had a pervasive impact upon participatory research in its various forms, from social action research within communities to action research within classrooms. Its appeal lies in the belief that, more so than any other research method, it has the potential to 'add value' to the participatory process because:

- it can be a powerful tool in the recruitment of potential participants;
- it eases access to the research process by creating a collaborative focus for joint work;
- it allows participants to provide accounts of their experiences in a form that they may find easier than written text;
- it can create spaces for dialogue between participants within research and between participants and the audiences for the research;
- it can lead to the production of a range of research outputs that meet the needs of participants and researchers.

This notion of 'adding value' is particularly popular when the research involves children and young people. A wide range of professionals and activists working with young people in recent years have increasingly acknowledged the importance of listening to their voices and treating them as actors with choices about what they do, when and how (Hadfield and Haw, 2000b, 2001). Part of this is due to a realisation that adults generating data about young people has the potential to distort their perspectives and experiences. The need, therefore, to offer young people creative ways of working together has almost inevitably led to adults looking towards new technologies. Ironically, by the time adults have identified what they consider to be a creative method such as video, young people have often moved on in their thinking about both what video is and what it can do. Making video films with young people about their issues is becoming more and more popular amongst adults for a number of reasons. They see young people being part of a culture in which it is relatively routine to upload thoughts and reflections onto YouTube, on a very wide range of subjects, from fashion and dance to self-harming and suicide, to provoke and specifically engage other young people in some form of dialogue. Their presentations can be contentious, controversial and 'hard hitting', mainly because they are free from adult intervention. They are also used to making their own short films using mobile phones and instantaneously distributing these to others, and this can be anything from filming one of their teachers late at night, 'out on the town', to gang violence and bullying, or simply filming an event such as a sleepover or a party. Adults and young people often live in cultures that operate with different sets of norms and expectations about video, which go beyond its consumption and production in various forms, from the slick, professional blockbuster, to the TV documentary-type film shown at various 'arty' film festivals, to the bite-sized offerings on the Internet.

In terms of the participatory research process, there are many examples of the use of video, with participants as researchers making films about an issue perceived as particularly applying to them and supported by others. The subject matter can be anything from homelessness, to campaigning for a skateboard park, to isolated communities making films about their everyday lives that they then show to similar communities. This last example refers to the pioneering work of Don Snowden, who worked with the small fishing communities of the Fogo Islands off the eastern coast of Newfoundland. By watching each other's films, these communities recognised that they shared similar problems and realised that, if they worked together, they could come up with some solutions (see Snowden, 2010). The use of video in this kind of project has become so commonplace that it has become recognised and labelled as a sub-group of participatory research, participatory video. Its methods are described as those that:

> vary from practitioner to practitioner, some choosing to keep the process more open, and others preferring to guide the subjects more, or even to wield the camera themselves. There is no fixed way in which PV [participatory video] has to be done, other than it involves the authorship of the group itself and that it be carried out in a truly participative and democratic way.
>
> (Lunch and Lunch, 2006, p. 11)

Although we have worked in this way ourselves and acknowledge that participatory video research projects have the potential for positive social change, empowerment and encouragement to take control of everyday lives, we would also argue that in isolation and if disconnected from broader social movements or groups of activists, such projects may achieve little in practice. The pitfalls of working with video in this way are many, and potentially disempowering. These pitfalls are to do with:

- raising expectations;
- lack of transparency about what the process can or will achieve;
- lack of follow-up;
- exploitation of the participatory approach to 'add value' to what is actually designed as a traditional research project;
- seeing video production as somehow an innately 'good' thing to be involved in.

'Handing over the video camera is not PV, and doing so without structure may cause great damage' (Lunch and Lunch, 2006, p. 4).

The point of this discussion is to draw attention to the interesting shift in the use of the terms 'participatory research' and 'participatory video'.

We do this because it highlights the tension we have previously identified, between video as process and video as product, which runs through a lot of work in this area. In considering this tension in Chapter 2, we explored differing notions of video as either primary or secondary data sources. The participatory 'twist' to this question concerns whether the video production process is the main source of data based on discussions between participants and researchers on the technical and creative aspects of the process, or whether the video product itself is the main source of data.

The previous brief discussions of the participatory process itself, and its various forms and incarnations, were sufficient to highlight that, in an approach that tries to balance the needs and agendas of the participants with the needs and agendas of the researchers, video can bring this tension into even sharper relief, for several reasons. First, as individuals become increasingly sophisticated in their media consumption, and it plays a stronger role in their self-construction, it influences their approach to video production. Researchers need to provide a complex mix of technical, creative and critical support to move individuals, and particularly young people, from consumers to producers of media. The impact of these forms of support and how they interact with the experiences of individuals as media consumers sets up methodological issues that range from questions of ownership to the authenticity of the video products. Second, those who have examined the methodological implications of the use of video have tended do so in areas of research other than participatory and have tended to do so as just one element of the research process, for example data collection, rather than its level of integration into the process (see Heath *et al.*, 2010). Unravelling the methodological issues that arise from this tension involves understanding the degree to which video is integrated into the research process. This, in turn, is dependent on decisions made about how each stage of the research process is going to proceed and the differing levels of participation involved.

The degree of integration of video within participatory research

Video is an important medium; it is easily transportable, inexpensive and is congruent with many young people's 'culture reading' skills. Unlike live performance (i.e. music, drama, dance etc.), it can be viewed more often than once, and can reach a potential audience larger than any auditorium maximum capacity. It was important that the medium for this project was video, given that it is a relevant cultural medium for the participants and for the intended audience.

(Howard *et al.*, 2002, p. 5)

The above quotation arises out of a 'peer research' project into young people's experience of the criminal justice system that integrated video production within the project:

Participants engaged simultaneously in two processes: a creative process (i.e. developing an idea from concept through to creative outcome, including developing skills in film-making), and an investigative process (researching and developing knowledge in subject matter).

(Howard *et al.*, 2002, p. 6)

The two quotations together hint at both the rationale for integration and the areas of the research process it is most likely to affect. Video is seen as appealing to young people (used in recruitment), it is a creative process, which fits in with young people's 'cultural reading skills' (data collection and analysis) and is a culturally relevant medium for the audience (creation of reports and dissemination).

The degree of integration of video within a participatory research process is not solely defined by the extent to which it is used within each stage. It also involves the extent to which video lies at the core of the research design. In the previous example, the two processes were seen to be running in parallel but distinct in nature, one creative, the other investigative. In a highly integrated project, there would be little distinction between the two processes, video production and research. Defining the nature of the video, its foci, audience and intended impact is similar to charting the research process, and the same depth of methodological and ethical consideration needs to be given to the video production process.

In a completely integrated approach, the video production process is the research process. The feel of both the video process and product would mirror the intentions and style of elements, data generation and reporting, within the same research 'genre'. Hence, a piece of 'critical' participatory research in which the video was highly integrated would result in a video production process and product that were as consciously self-critical and critiquing as any written materials.

Until comparatively recently, a high degree of integration was rare and often the province of those who came from a strong media-studies or creative-arts background and had moved into research or who had worked within research genres where video has had a long history. A good example here is the work of Dirk Schouten (Schouten, 2010). His work is based on a three-stage model, to divide what he describes 'as a complex job into separately manageable stages'. The model is based around research, analysis and production stages. Although each stage is subdivided even further, in practice they blend together and at times run concurrently. The research stage is broken down into knowledge assessment, problem definition and choice of theme. The analysis stage marks the shift from research into production. Analysis is based on the conversations around materials and insights generated in the earlier stage. From this analysis, a thesis and a choice of medium emerge, and this leads to the production stage, based on a shooting schedule and list of things to record and film. In these instances, the methodological issues that arise do so as much from the juxtaposition of video and research as they do from within either tradition.

Our own participatory research with video has primarily been with young people, around relatively contentious issues, and this has meant we have had to consider our own positions quite frequently and very critically. This positioning has not just been about understanding the practical demands of the work, but also involved a theoretical consideration of the methodological and ethical issues that arise from the juxtaposition of our construction of participatory research, the usage of 'video' and working with these participants on the sensitive issues being researched.

Our reflections concerning these issues have centred on a series of methodological and ethical questions, such as:

• Are there distinct issues that arise specifically because of the interactions of video, participatory research and 'ordinary people', particularly young people?
• Are there issues of such significance in any of these three areas that they defined/dominated the nature of these interactions?
• Which of these issues, or combination of these, have most affected the form of projects being undertaken and presented the greatest challenges to the researcher?

These sorts of question raised even more philosophical questions, such as:

• Is there such a thing as an epistemology of video that is recognised, or being developed, in these projects, and is it creating a distinct methodology with its own set of challenges?
• Are there uniquely powerful methodological issues, because they have cultural resonance within certain research areas or organisations, or

present technically specific challenges, connected with any of these themes, which transcend their contextualisation and interaction?

Our approach to considering these challenges is a three 'dimensions' model (see Figure 5.1), based on the three strands that have defined our own research area:

1 The video dimension: This dimension ranges from video being mentioned as an element of the project to projects where it is fully integrated. What we mean by integrated is discussed in the next section, but essentially relates to the video process running in parallel and crossing over with the research process in order to achieve its aims.

2 The participatory dimension: This reflects the power relationships between young people and the researchers. At one end of the dimension are those projects in which young people take the lead, or at least achieve some equality of control, and, at the other end, are those where the researchers may actively involve them, but in which they have little say over its development. Here, the dimension ranges from their essentially acting as a resource of insights, to being co-researchers and to being supported/developed as lead researchers.

3 The agenda/outcomes dimension: Here, the distinction is between projects where the main aim or agenda is about benefits for young people and those that are more concerned with achieving the agenda of the researcher. At one end of the dimension would be projects trying to achieve specific concrete changes that would benefit young people or to provide them with some form of educational gain, including insights into their own self-understanding or even knowledge about video production. At the other end are those projects where it is the interest of the researcher in understanding more about an aspect of young people's lives that dominates.

Positioning your participatory project

Our starting point for each new project is to revisit our position on each of the three dimensions of our model, as each offers different possibilities and presents new problems. How we position ourselves determines how we practically use video within the project. The remainder of this chapter focuses on these practical issues. We focus on three issues that are strongly foregrounded by any project attempting to use video to generate participation:

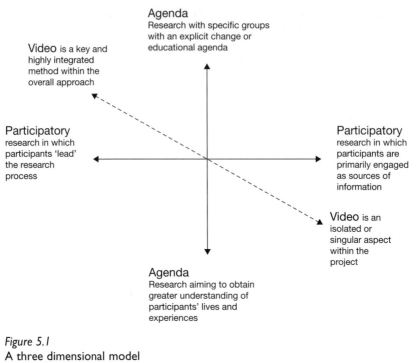

Figure 5.1
A three dimensional model
of participatory video

recruitment and access, negotiating the focus of the research and managing relationships. Other key stages within a project, such as designing and presenting the finished video(s), are considered in the following, linked chapter on video and the articulation of voice.

The practical issues associated with using video to generate participation in research

In discussing these issues from a more practical perspective, we want to refer to two of our projects, Urbanfields and 'Seen but not heard'. Urbanfields was part of an ESRC Priority Network, 'Pathways into and out of crime: risk, resilience and diversity'. This consisted of five projects, each looking at different aspects of the involvement of young people with at-risk behaviours, from experiences with drugs, exclusion from school or having a parent or significant other serving a prison sentence, to living in a difficult and specific community. The focus for the research was to understand more about the social processes around risk and resilience. The aim was to support young people in articulating their perspective by focusing on their agency and, through this, to develop a theoretical critique of a debate dominated in criminology by notions of the predictive power of 'risk factors' and inter-vention strategies – so-called 'risk factorology' (Kemshall, 2003). We regarded this approach as important because, in criminology, the coupling of the notion of a criminal career with the causality behind risk and protection has given rise to the notion of a pathway into and out of crime. The internal logic of the pathway has encouraged researchers and practitioners to search for risk and protective factors that could be affected by interventions prior to offending and to guide 'treatments' afterwards, leading to greater and greater efforts to predict offending behaviour and to legitimate earlier and earlier interventions in young people's lives (Haw, 2006a, 2010b). This has occurred without a great deal of consideration of the negative consequences of the associated monitoring and interventions on both young people's civil liberties and the professional practices of those running the criminal justice system.

The 'Seen but not heard' project was funded by the Joseph Rowntree Foundation. We worked with a group of young people who had been excluded from school. This group worked as co-researchers with a university-based team, some of their teachers and a small team of youth workers, to make a video targeted at the school management to tell them what it felt like to be excluded from their school and to get them to reconsider their policies and practices. Their completed video was a mixture of interviews and role play presented in a news-based format. Initially, the group planned to screen the video to four key audiences: a selection of staff at their school, local head teachers, governors and the Chief Education Officer of the LEA. Their intentions were twofold: to have their voice heard clearly in a debate about these issues, and to encourage teachers and officials to be more sensitive to the needs of young people when tackling the joint problems of exclusion and non-attendance. They wanted to provide a critical voice that would challenge the perceptions of professionals about excluded pupils.

Urbanfields: recruiting participants, negotiating research foci and developing a mulitimodal approach to video

Urbanfields was our name for a community that was chosen as a place to carry out the research with young people and their 'risk repertoires', because it was one of the first areas in Britain to be routinely patrolled by armed police after dark and has a reputation across the city, built up over several generations, for its gang and drug cultures. The region in which Urbanfields is located features among the top four most dangerous British places to live in terms of gun crime (Povey and Kaiza, 2005, p. 49). It also has very specific boundaries, but is connected by a bridge to a wealthy suburb populated by 'middle-class' professionals owing to the reputation of its schools. A number of the young people from Urbanfields now go to these schools because of the closure of the only secondary school in Urbanfields.

The project worked with six groups of young people aged between eleven and twenty-one. One of these groups was made up entirely of young men of Asian origin, and another of young women of a similar age, of Afro-Caribbean descent. The four remaining groups were younger and more mixed in terms of gender and ethnic background. In total, there were between fifty and seventy participants, although the number is significantly reduced if only those who worked to the completion of their video are counted. All the participants had a combination of risk factors that identified them as potential offenders. Some of them were, or became, drawn into the criminal justice system during the life of the research. At least two of the group were arrested for involvement in serious criminal activity, including grievous bodily harm and murder, and several others were the recipients of Anti-Social Behaviour Orders. Our research involved working with these young people on quite sensitive subjects, and so video was seen as a means of accessing their views, without 'frightening off' participants through intrusive personal questioning. Researchers from the project also worked with, and serially interviewed, sixteen adults, representing a range of services, who worked within Urbanfields. These were the police, social workers, youth offending team workers, probation officers, community drugs workers, youth workers and teachers. The final outcomes of the research were two trigger films, six films made by the young people themselves and a final DVD created by the research team. Data generation occurred over three phases.

The recruitment, access and entry phase began with interviews with professionals about their personal theories of risk and resilience. These views were incorporated into a short trigger video that combined footage of the area, discussions with young people about the local area, and local and national media coverage of violent events in Urbanfields. We have discussed what we mean by a trigger video and how to go about making one more fully in Chapter 3. This trigger video was used in the recruitment process by being shown at a range of venues in the community. At times, members of the team were present, whereas, at others, it was shown by local community workers. The team produced a one-page leaflet to accompany the trigger video, outlining in everyday language what the research was about, why we were doing it and how we hoped to go about it. The leaflets were pushed through letterboxes and left in local shops and clubs. We also set out to recruit local community-based researchers, and the trigger tape was used at our first meeting, in a community centre, with people who had extensive family ties in the area, hoping that at least some of them might be interested in supporting our work.

The trigger tape was designed so that it contrasted an 'outsider' view of the community, from the perspective of professionals who rarely lived in the area and from the local media, with an 'insider' view, as presented by young people and a few well-known local characters. The professionals and media, for very different reasons, tended to see the community through the dominant discourse of risk factors and high levels of crime. The video also embodied aspects of the criminal justice system many of the young people would had come into contact with, from the risk assessment forms used to assess their levels of risk-taking, to shots of local police officers. It showed how the local media often stereotyped them as potential delinquent 'hoodies'. Most importantly, however, it challenged them to consider how they would like to portray their lives and their communities, by discussing the risks they took and why.

The trigger tape had to establish a number of things simultaneously about the project and the project team. It had to demonstrate that we had some understanding of:

- the differences between how the community was seen by outsiders and how it actually felt to live in it;
- how young people might view and construct risk differently from adults and the professionals they came across in their everyday lives;
- that there was no single experience of living in Urbanfields, and that, literally and symbolically, people's experiences were fragmented.

This meant capturing contradictory views, juxtaposing these and highlighting tensions and differences. The trigger tape also had to be short and snappy, no more than ten minutes, and to engage attention, and so well-known, local figures and landmarks that prompted recognition among the audience were used.

The project made extensive use of community-based researchers, who supported the core research team. The main recruitment criterion for these researchers was that they lived in Urbanfields. They were recruited because of the nature of the local community and the difficulty in engaging young people within research that could involve looking at their involvement in crime. Five community researchers eventually agreed to take part in the project. Their training in the use of video and other research techniques was part of the project design. These community-based researchers were working in potentially dangerous situations, on sensitive subjects, within a community in which they were known. This required the development of a number of protocols to support them and ensure their safety. Their role as part of the research team was to provide an insider's view of the happenings within Urbanfields, encouragement and support to the young people and advice on ethical aspects to do with preserving anonymity and confidentiality.

Each of the six groups was given a broad brief within which to negotiate the focus of their video. We were interested in them presenting a view of Urbanfields that they felt represented their lives. We did not explicitly focus on risk and risk-taking in the brief, on the basis that, as groups of young people within this community, it would be difficult for them not to touch upon issues and areas that overlapped with our interests. At the end of the project, these videos were to be owned and used by them in whichever way they saw fit. We also provided a venue in which each film could be 'premièred', and a number of prizes were awarded for categories such as Best Film and Funniest Film.

We could be relatively sanguine about negotiating a focus, as the content of their videos was of less interest to us than the discussions that occurred while each film was edited and produced. Each week, we would set up a mini-editing suite in one of the local youth clubs and work with the young people on their ideas and the materials they were filming. These sessions were tape-recorded and filmed by the research team to give us our second layer of data. The footage collected by the researchers over this phase, together with elements of the tape-recorded discussions, were then incorporated into the original trigger video to make a second trigger video for use in the next phase of the research. The selection of material in this second trigger was now based upon the themes that had arisen from the young people, juxtaposed with voice-overs from young people and professionals. This trigger tape would now be shown to groups of professional and young people, so that they could respond to the issues it raised in a series of focus groups and individual interviews.

How then did we select the themes that had arisen as the young people made and edited their videos? As the participants discussed their videos, several key urban 'mythologies' emerged around their risk-taking and the behaviour of others. These mythologies included drug dealing and the lifestyle surrounding it, gang violence, notions of 'territory' and rivalry, sexual relationships and the status of being the 'number one' girl. It became clear that some participants were talking from direct experiences, whereas others were talking from either indirect experiences or from a 'wannabe' perspective. These broad mythologies in part functioned to rationalise and normalise some of the more extreme aspects of living in Urbanfields. Some of these myths were linked to events within the community, for example the appearance of graffiti around the estate proclaiming 'Charlie why ya hideing', which was linked to a dispute between two drug dealers over a woman.

The second trigger tape picked up on this and other explicit references as a way of exploring the urban mythologies that shaped the young people's experiences. As these filmed materials were viewed over the various phases of the research, different audiences commented on the myths, making them a good source of reflection, as they were often interpreted differently. In terms of developing a more critical and reflective reading on what was occurring in the community, they became important for several reasons, particularly because they allowed the research to focus on difficult and sensitive issues that 'lived' in a community where there were a lot of tensions around drug dealing and gang violence. Discussing the myths around the graffiti allowed for a discussion of already processed events and created a safe place for collective reflection. In a piece of research dealing with difficult and sensitive issues, where there was a great deal of tension around what could and could not be talked about, the myths provided a space to discuss and 'play' with wider issues.

In terms of the second aim, to encourage a reflexive awareness of the agency of the participants, the myths circulating around the graffiti were also important because they lived sufficiently within the locality for a range of participants and professionals to be aware of them and to hold different understandings of them. The production and consumption phases of the video process were helpful in focusing on, and accounting for, the agency of the participants, by allowing for discussions on the extent to which they rejected or took on board these myths and, therefore, used them in the construction of their own contexts.

As the participants made numerous decisions about the content of their videos, their 'internal narratives', spaces for critical subjectivity, were opened up, reflecting their broader agency. Crucially though, as these videos were produced and shown to different audiences, the potential to enhance this reflexivity and criticality was developed. This is because images bring with them an analysis of their internal narrative, through critical engagement with how successfully they convey its story, and an 'external narrative' as the audience reacts to this content. Social relations of visual images are therefore key to understanding their meaning, because they are the product of individual action set within a nexus of social contexts and their interconnections.

Getting the participants to engage with collectively held myths, such as those of 'the gangsta', the dealer, the gang member, the 'number one' girl, in their own videos involved incorporating elements, within the video process, of what they considered ordinary and everyday within their locality with what was perceived as extraordinary by those outside it, and exploring why this was so. An exploration of these mythologies relied on the collective experience of the participants and professionals. In this way, the internal and external narratives of the different videos revealed through the production and consumption processes also highlighted the connections between the 'felt' worlds of the participants and how they then fed these back into the wider social discourses operating around them.

Methodologically, the Urbanfields project, and the way video was used within it, proved to be a useful way of generating participation on a number of levels. First, it had the potential to support participants to reflect on aspects of lives perceived to be everyday and mundane, as well as the more dramatic, difficult and potentially painful. Second, it had the potential to encourage a reflexive awareness of agency at certain moments, and how this might change, as they discussed similar situations such as reactions to the 'Charlie' graffiti. Third, it exposed the linkages between internal, personal, 'felt' narratives and the external, social discourses, through its intrinsic internal and external narrative arcs as it was created and viewed. Last, it allowed the research to focus on difficult and sensitive issues that lived in a community where there were a lot of tensions around drug dealing and gang violence. As a community myth, the 'Charlie' graffiti reflected the application of wider social discourses to specific events within Urbanfields, which then took on their own mythic status. In this sense, the graffiti were a reflection of events that had already been processed, creating a safe place for collective reflection because they were part of common parlance. Taken in combination, these reasons meant that video had the potential to access the emotional aspects of individual lives, because of its unique potential to develop critical subjectivity through reflection, reflexivity and criticality, and, used in this way, it generated multiple levels of participation.

Managing different relationships throughout the participatory process

In the 'Seen but not heard' project, we had six months to work with a group of young people, around a focus of our choosing that fitted in with a theme set by the funders, that of 'raising the voice of young people in preventive work with families'. Essentially, this project was to be a piece of participative research, drawing on our experiences of educational and social action research in a number of settings (Hadfield and Bennett, 1995). We began work by looking for a partnership with an organisation that was already working with a group of young people. We considered several programmes before eventually choosing one, which we will call the 'Time out' programme, run by a local community organisation called 'The Edge', on a local peripheral housing estate. This programme was working with a group of young people who were excluded, or at risk of being excluded, from school.

The project had an articulated agenda, to develop the voice of the group, so that their experience of being excluded would be heard, not only by their school, but also by the broad range of professionals with whom they came into contact. In particular, we wanted to get their views heard on issues such as:

- how they had come to be at risk of being excluded from school;
- their families' feelings about the preventive strategies they were involved in;
- the impact of being targeted by multiple agencies.

We decided to work with this group because it had several important features:

- The school (in partnership with 'The Edge') had already established the group in an innovative move, as a means of positively engaging with these young people.
- 'The Edge' worked closely with the school over a range of its activities and had credibility with the young people living in the area.
- The 'Time out' team told us that the young men were familiar with discussing sensitive issues and working in small groups.

Our role was to create a research process that was intrinsically worthwhile for the young men, to help them make a video product that they 'owned' and that had the potential to change the views and actions of professionals, and to get it viewed by their chosen audience. The young men wanted to have an influence on the decision-making processes within their school, and particularly their approach to dealing with pupils at risk of exclusion. We asked the group to nominate a 'safe' teacher who would work with them throughout the making of the video and advise them of the likely reactions of their chosen audience. We recruited this teacher, with the permission of the head teacher, to work with the young men and us during school hours.

In addition, we approached a range of people involved with school exclusion in the local education authority and secured their involvement as an audience for the video.

We had several research relationships to maintain: between the school and ourselves; between the 'Time out' team and ourselves; and between the 'Time out' team and the school. At the same time, we also needed to establish a relationship with the young men that would not harm the existing relationship that they had with the 'Time out' workers. We did this partly by attending social events with the group throughout the lifetime of the project.

Working with and supporting the 'Time out' team

We agreed with the 'Time out' team that we would have regular debriefing sessions with them about the research, especially as they were actively involved in the work and had particular insights into the experiences, circumstances and relationships within the group of young men. Sometimes, these debriefing sessions concentrated on practical issues (such as transport, administration or the location of activities), and sometimes they were more concerned with group dynamics, the strengths and weaknesses of the research or links between the project and the school.

The first tension we experienced was in making the most of these sessions, especially in the critical early stages of the research, when we had to rely on their 'insider' knowledge of the young men. We all had other demands on our time, and working with the group in the morning was exhausting for both the 'Time out' team and ourselves. In addition to gleaning more information about the young men in the programme in these sessions, we also touched on aspects of the team's work with schools. They expressed their desire to be more flexibly integrated into a range of school activities. We knew from our discussions with the school, however, that the activities of the 'Time out' team did not always meet with approval. Some staff felt that pupils' attendance at the programme was effectively a 'reward for bad behaviour', and that it consisted of too many 'outings' and not enough 'work'. One teacher was pleasantly surprised when we described the detail and depth of the activities that the group was engaged in as part of the research project. Similarly, staff at 'The Edge' were not always aware of the ways in which the school perceived them. Dealing with these differences in perceptions and agendas between partner organisations was the basis of the next series of tensions we experienced.

Working with and supporting the school

Implicit in the design of the project was an intention to work with the school on issues identified by the young men. However, we always knew that this was going to be a difficult task. The school had a history of decline and intervention, it had not done well in its recent Ofsted inspection and it was attempting to tackle a number of 'serious weaknesses' identified by the inspectors. The inspection report stated that 'To remedy the serious weaknesses the school needs to raise standards of attainment, improve the quality of management and raise levels of attendance.' By the time we began the research, the school had an action plan in place, based on four key issues detailed in the inspection report. There were also a number of other initiatives taking place at the school, for example: a targeted literacy programme, a focused effort on the achievement of current Year 11 pupils and pastoral work with younger pupils aimed at improving attendance in later years.

All this, in our opinion, had made the school an important institution to work with, but, at the same time, made it more difficult to liaise with and support the school. We hoped, in particular, that the school would welcome the opportunity to listen to the voices of some of its excluded pupils. At the beginning of the project, the acting head teacher and the head of Year 11 both agreed to be interviewed and to respond to their research statement. It was also encouraging when the 'safe' drama teacher was given permission to be involved in the project. But our optimism was ill founded. By the time the video was finished, the school had been placed in 'special measures', and the voice of Ofsted began to silence more marginalised perspectives.

The signs that the school was starting to turn inwards on itself and becoming less willing to listen to voices other than the voice of Ofsted started to emerge when the young men set about interviewing the managers of the school. The young people who conducted the interviews with the acting head teacher and the head of Year 11 were more than a little reticent about doing so. Partly for this reason, they asked if they could interview them at the drop-in centre, but in the event both members of staff were interviewed in school. The young people, supported by members of the research team, were expected to take the lead in preparing and conducting these interviews. Even with support, they were noticeably quiet and unchallenging in their approach to these teachers, who in turn adopted a very different stance to the one we had encountered at the outset of the project. The presence of the video camera was referred to during the interviews by both teachers, and it is fair to say that their answers were given in the knowledge that they might become public statements about the school and be used to form judgements about its staff, pupils and achievements. In particular, they avoided questions that implied criticisms of teachers, tended to turn these into criticisms of pupils, and claimed not to have enough knowledge to comment on several of the issues raised by the young people.

As the research progressed, working with the school became fraught with difficulties. The sheer pressures of years of inspection and reinspection, of being subjected to 'special measures', of declining staff morale and a battered reputation rendered the school almost inaccessible. As an organisation, it had become so overwhelmed with externally imposed change it had become less able to cope with internally generated change from its own pupils and staff. With the appointment of a new head teacher, it became harder to make contact with the right person by phone, by letter or in person.

We now faced a number of tensions and dilemmas. To what extent should we push forward the research process before the school closed itself off completely? The danger was that we would effectively hijack the research process from the young men. How should we mediate between the young men and the school about the composition of the final video product? Through the research process, the young men had become increasingly vehement about the way in which they had been treated, but the school seemed less and less able to cope with a highly critical video. If we tried to lessen its criticality, would we be drawn into 'cooling out' the young men? To what extent could the research team and workers from 'The Edge' use their influence with the school, without adversely affecting their ongoing relationships with staff there?

Working with, and supporting, the young men

The work began well, with the young men enthusiastically deciding to whom they were going to speak and what they were going to film. Their list of people they wanted to talk to and video included senior education welfare officers, head teachers, their head of year, school governors and representatives from large local employers. The model of video production that we were working with focused on making a video that was both critical and reflective, rather than just the technicalities of the process. It aimed to open up issues from the perspective of the young men and bounce them around the different professional groups that worked with them.

We worked with the young men to get them to think about the process of change within an organisation such as a school and what kind of material could initiate change. Eventually, they decided to create a video that would represent their views, but could also be shown to their teachers as part of a staff development event on pupils who had been excluded or who were at risk of exclusion. We discussed with them what kind of balance they wanted to strike, between being critical of how they had been treated and getting teachers to change how they behaved and thought about school exclusions.

Several of the researchers had successfully used this video method before with in-service youth workers (Hadfield and Jardine, 1997) and in a number of educational settings (Schouten and Watling, 1997). This, though, was the first time that we had worked in such an in-depth way with a group that had come together because of how they had been treated and categorised by others. This, and the instability of the young men's lives, amplified a number of tensions within a process that required them to have both creative and technical control over what was happening.

As the work progressed, the impact of these limited experiences of the young men in expressing their 'critical voice' on the creative process became clearer. We needed continually to readjust our involvement in the creative process so as to give increasing control to the group as their expertise developed. We concentrated our inputs on:

- encouraging them to put their voices more up front in the video and to do this in an increasing variety of forms;
- keeping them in touch with their original ideas, so that they did not become swamped with the issues raised by the professional they were interviewing;
- providing them with as much time and space as possible to reflect on the new issues their work kept uncovering, while completing other parts of the video, to maintain their motivation.

The creative aspects of video production interact continuously with the technical, and so we also needed to make adjustments in how we supported them in this area. Here we focused our advice on:

- coping with the large amount of video material they had collected by making a group decision about the overall structure for the video and then giving smaller groups responsibility for the editing of individual sections;
- increasing their confidence with different forms of filming so that they moved away from 'talking heads' shots of professional discussions.

In our work with the young men, possibly the single biggest challenge we faced was how we dealt with the existing beliefs the group held about themselves. Over their time on the programme, they had developed a 'group think', a number of perspectives that had become self-supporting and crucial to maintaining their resistance to what was happening to them at school. We discuss this issue more fully in Chapter 6.

Managing these relationships, like hosting a good party, was a time-consuming and emotionally draining experience that was both costly and rewarding. Like some parties, it may be that it is better appreciated in retrospect. What it highlighted was the duality of video: while as a product and process it brought together the group internally, it came to be threatening to those outside it, its audience. These issues are dealt with more fully in the following chapter. In retrospect, as we tried to balance the agendas of the very different guests at this party, we perhaps did so at the expense of their enjoyment.

In concluding this chapter, we would emphasise our belief that the use of video to generate participation is methodologically unique in the world of video research, because of the complexity of these projects and their broader relevance. This is owing to the interactions of three factors:

- the dynamics of the collaborative relationships between researchers, practitioners and participants;
- the integration of a distinct technical and creative process, video production, within the overall participatory research process;
- the intention to impact on a wide range of audiences by presenting the perceptions and attitudes of individuals in a variety of formats.

The range and depth of its potential benefit are the major reasons behind the degree of methodological experimentation in the use of video within participatory research and its growing popularity. Within the discussion in this chapter, there are specific gaps. These are to do with the ethical issues that can arise from dealing with contentious issues within the lives of young people, highlighted specifically by the Urbanfields project to do with drug usage and other criminal activities. Mainly, these concerns revolve around issues of power inherent in any research relationships, and by that we mean for both researchers and participants. Following from this, then, is the issue of using voice as a construct underpinning this work, and that of the limitations and potential of video to place different, and often contrasting, voices in the kinds of dialogue that can promote criticality and reflection. It is these issues that are the focus of Chapter 6. The second gap is concerned with methodological issues arising from the design and evaluation of texts intended to change the opinions and actions of others, such as professionals who work with young people, and the broader analytical potential of video-based texts created by young people to provide a means of researching their lives and cultures. These issues are explored more fully in Chapter 3.

**DANGER
STEEP DECLINE
IN PARTICIPATION
AHEAD**

Chapter 6

Video, voice and articulation

The questions of voice and participation are increasingly global concerns for policy-makers and practitioners. Inclusive policies and practices that reflect the needs and aspirations of service users and local communities are seen as means of ensuring a fair distribution of opportunities and outcomes for a wide range of excluded or under-represented groups. These are seen as particularly relevant issues within inner-city communities marked by wide-scale exclusion and for those specific groups most in danger of not being heard. The development of innovative research approaches that support the articulation of these silenced groups has come about because of a need to take into account their different epistemological standpoints, issues of equity and power, and dynamic models of identity formation and representation. Video has been at the forefront of many of these developments, as it has been constructed as an 'articulation technology' that is democratic, em-powering and persuasive in nature. In this chapter, we concentrate on supporting young people in articulating their voice, as it brings into sharp relief the key constructs that need to be grappled with. The project we are going to use to highlight these issues is the 'Seen but not heard' project, where we worked with a group of young people to make a video about school exclusion.

The root metaphor

Our preferred root metaphor for thinking about the role of video and the articulation of voice is that of a good pop song. In this metaphor, the researcher is the record producer, the project is the song and the participants are the recording group. A good pop song will be remembered because it is 'catchy' – a memorable tune that can be interpreted by different people on many levels, because the simplicity and honesty of its lyrics mean that they can be invested with meanings from the deep and mysterious to the more everyday, depending on the empathy and context of the listener. Finally, it will be enduring if its quality and appeal mean that it stands the test of time and maintains its relevance. The song, once produced, has to be disseminated through different media to ensure that it is heard by as wide a range of audiences as possible. The choice of this metaphor is not a flippant one: popular music has long been the preferred means of cultural expression for many excluded groups and a means of protest, ranging from the highly political to the very personal.

What do we mean by voice?

In order to explore the role of video in the articulation of voice and to discuss its potential, and limitations, we need first of all to come to some agreement as to what we mean by voice by exploring some of the commonsense assumptions and linking these to different types of voice. Voice, whether articulated or embedded within actions or artefacts, is a constant issue within the participatory research process. Researchers are positioned as 'outsiders' and 'insiders' as they move across various cultural, political and organisational boundaries (Haw, 1996, 1998), raising issues about who is heard and what is heard, what is listened to and how it is listened to. Whether it is a white researcher running focus groups within black communities, or a community activist creating professional development materials for policy-makers, the complexity and fluidity of participatory research highlights the limited nature of much of the current discussion of voice. At least within the UK context, voice has become increasingly linked with participation in civic life, local decision-making and improvements to public services, making more individualistic and passive notions of voice increasingly less relevant. As voice in the UK has become an established element of central and local government rhetoric, this has opened it up to questions and criticisms over whether the focus of working with the voice of young people should be on supporting young people articulate their own voice or directed towards responding to the issues of adults and professionals and eliciting a response from them.

Four key themes run through much of the literature on voice. The first is that voice privileges experience, over theory or training, as the basis of the understanding of an issue or activity. This privileging of experience fundamentally relies on the notion of 'interior authenticity' as the basis of the validity of the voice being expressed. The second theme is the privileging of the excluded, silenced or subordinate voices, over dominant voices, to initiate and guide change. This raises concerns over the appropriateness of existing mechanisms to facilitate the voice of those already marginalised and ignored. The third theme is that voice as an inclusive idea recognises the proliferation of different voices and the fragmented nature of experiences and understanding. As the validity of any voice relates to its inner authenticity, rather than being validated by the warrant of those who are listening to it, then it becomes the responsibility of the audience to judge the voice on its own terms and not their own. This idea provides the link to the fourth and final theme, that voice is intertwined with notions of activism, representation and empowerment. All four themes coalesce around what makes a particular voice worth listening to, how to get it heard, and finally how to make sure it is responded to.

If you are interested in using video to help a group articulate their voice, then you need to familiarise yourself with some of the commonsense assumptions people make about it and, on this basis, come to your own understanding of the main arguments about why it is seen as important or not. In this instance, we are going to look at four key assumptions, and these are all related to working with young people, although you can easily substitute the specific group you are intending to work with:

- The voice of young people is important because it is based on their experience.
- Young people can tell professionals about their experiences in a way that is meaningful and will help them understand more about young people.
- Professionals have few opportunities to hear young people.
- Young people can get things changed by getting their voices heard.

We unpick each assumption in turn by putting forward alternative arguments and perspectives. We want to show how each of these assumptions has been challenged in the debate surrounding the worth of the voice of young people, because this is key to understanding both the popularity of using video when working with young people and its usefulness. These challenges range from the practical to the more philosophical in nature. All we can do in this section is highlight some of the main criticisms of these assumptions and give you a broad framework to examine critically what others have said.

Assumption 1: The voice of young people is important because it is based on their experience

Probably the most fundamental assumption made about the voice of young people is:

- We should listen to it because it is the voice of experience. Only young people can really know 'how it is' to be a young person at this particular time, in this particular community, as a member of this youth club, as a pupil in this school.

This leads us on to two further assumptions:

- Young people hold their particular views and opinions because of the specific nature of their experiences as young people.
- Together, their experiences and beliefs give them a particular way of looking at the world around, which creates a 'young people's perspective'.

It is the combination of their unique experiences, beliefs and opinions, and their outlook, which makes it so worthwhile to listen to young people.

The main challenges to this assumption have their roots in the historical development of how young people have been viewed by society as a whole. The central question is, to what extent do young people know and see things differently, not because of their experience, but because they have less mature or sophisticated and realistic understandings of 'how things are'. In its extreme form, this view has been used to silence the viewpoints of young people. It was not worth listening to them because they had not developed the cognitive skills and abilities to make any 'real' sense of the world. As this view has become more discredited, sometimes owing to the tragic consequences of ignoring young people, professionals are left to struggle with their recognition that young people may hold certain views because of a lack of experience and skills, rather than because of having a unique insight. This issue often comes down to the extent to which professionals are happy to work with the 'natural' voice of young people, or whether they prefer to develop a more informed or critical voice. Young people hold their particular views and opinions because of the specific nature of their experiences as young people.

A key criticism of this assumption concerns the extent to which the views of young people are their own, in the sense of being based on their experience, and the extent to which they are influenced by the views and agendas of others. It touches on the debate about how 'natural' the opinions are that we get from young people, but also raises additional questions about the power of others to shape the perceptions of a young generation. Like adults, young people form their opinions on the basis of the social norms and values that surround them, as well as their experiences, although they can be seen as particularly susceptible to certain forms of manipulation because of the specific power relationships in which they are caught up. This view can be used to invalidate the voice of young people.

The question here is the extent to which young people are given the opportunity to define their own perspectives in the process of articulating themselves. This is often discussed in terms of the extent to which the power relationships shift in the process of articulation. This shift is from a situation in which young people receive their rights via the adults who care and provide for them, to ones in which they have the capacity to exercise their rights on the basis of being recognised as equal to other groups in society. Here, it is helpful to look at the distinction that Beresford and Croft (1993) make between approaches that put young people in very different power relationships. They dichotomise these approaches between those that are consumerist and those that are democratic.

A democratic approach moves beyond seeing young people simply as consumers of services to include involvement in wider decision-making and the change process. As consumers, they have limited rights, and the only power they may have is to choose not to use a service, to vote with their feet. In a democratic approach, they have a more developed set of rights, but with them come various responsibilities. For some, these responsibilities include a commitment to becoming more aware of where their views come from and being critical of these origins. In a very real sense, young people tend to be asked to earn rights that are often simply given to adults.

Together, the experiences and beliefs of young people give them a particular way of looking at the world from which they create a 'young person's outlook' on life. Their lives and experiences are at least as diverse as those of other social groups. When we set out to listen to their voice as young people, we need to recognise that being young is only part of what creates this perspective. They are also young men and women, they come from different ethnic and social-class backgrounds, live in different family structures and come from a range of communities. This brings us back to the assumption about the primacy of their experience and the specific insights they have. The question is: how specific and unique a set of experiences should we be looking at? The experiences of young, working-class Muslim women may have very little in common with the experiences of middle-class, rural young men. At one level, this fragmentation raises technical questions about how representative or inclusive a sample of young people is. In certain cases, where the voice sought is very specific, fragmentation may not be an issue. At a more fundamental level, it can challenge the validity of the idea of there being a young persons' perspective. It raises questions about whether we do young people a service in raising their voice, in isolation from others in their community. Would it not be better to raise their voice in combination with their families or other groups of young people?

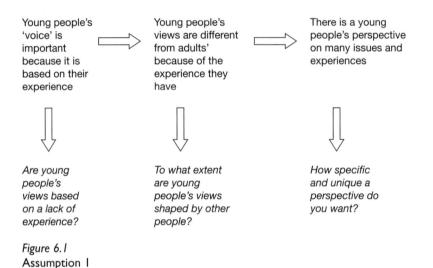

Figure 6.1
Assumption 1

Assumption 2: Young people can tell professionals about their experiences in a way that is meaningful and will help them understand more about young people

Young people are not asked to voice simply for their own good, although a number of personal benefits are claimed for them in doing so. Rather, they are being given the opportunity to do so because people believe they can learn from what they are saying. A fundamental assumption, then, about voice is that:

• Young people can relate their experiences in a way that is meaningful to and useful for adults.

Along with this basic assumption come two others:

- Young people need help to articulate their views effectively.
- Young people are in the best position to talk about being young.

The issue with this assumption is not so much about whether young people will or will not make sense, but rather what kind of meaning young people will set out to create in the process of giving voice. The phenomenon of adults being told what they want or expect to hear is well known among professionals working with young people on behalf of the courts or social services. Of course, this effect is not restricted to young people, and it is a two-way process. Adults, too, position themselves differently in a variety of social relationships, including their interactions with young people and children. Researchers and professionals working with young people are complicit in this 'story-telling'. It is, therefore, not something that can be eliminated, but, rather, something that it is important to manage as part of a process. Interviews are often described as 'tales told to tourists'; to an extent, you cannot avoid some of this, and possibly the best way of thinking about this is to ask yourself 'What kind of tourist do I want to be?' and 'What kind of stories do I want to hear?'

One way of looking at the assumption that young people need help to articulate their views effectively is to consider that this arises because adults fail to understand that they are already giving voice, but in ways that adults don't recognise. At this point, especially if we are considering the use of video, we should ask ourselves if voice is just about words, and consider the degree to which their views can be adequately expressed through talk alone. Do we undervalue the other ways young people can express themselves, for example through behaviour, clothes, music, apathy, loyalty and, just as importantly, silence? Power attaches to particular modes of expression, and often this can serve to exclude particular groups, including young people. Research and policy-making narrowly based on verbally articulate participants will necessarily fail to include the views of people expressed in other ways, and so video has some obvious advantages over other media. However, young people can be doubly disadvantaged in this regard since, as mentioned earlier, it is often assumed they have not yet developed the capacity to express themselves in the way required to exercise their rights.

Researchers and professionals are often in the position of having to balance the fact that young people know a lot about 'being young' with their own concern that they might be blinkered about the limits of this knowledge, especially with regard to their understanding of other young people's lives.

In working to achieve a suitable balance, we think the issue of authenticity, which we have developed in the next section, is of crucial importance. We do not think that there can be a simple formula to follow here; there should, however, be some means of challenging the working assumption that it is possible to develop an 'objective' representation of the differing views and experiences of young people.

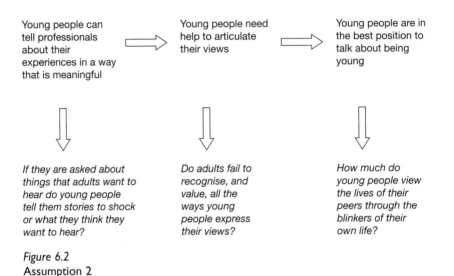

Figure 6.2
Assumption 2

Assumption 3: Professionals have few opportunities to hear young people

The growing interest in voice is partially premised on the assumption that many professionals are distanced from young people – a distance that comes about because they have limited contact with them, or the kind of contact they have means there is little opportunity for them to listen to the views and opinions of young people. The assumption is that:

• Professionals have few opportunities to hear young people.

This leads on to further sets of assumptions about the kind of voice professionals, and in some cases politicians, prefer to listen to, and the need for specific innovations to make that happen:

- Professionals will listen to a representative and considered voice from young people.
- Young people require their own structures and specifically designed processes to help them get their voice heard.

The issue here is not so much about whether this assumption is true or not, bearing in mind what has already been discussed about the failure of people to recognise different forms of voice, but rather why this situation has come about. Is it owing to overworked professionals having insufficient time? Do people need more and better training to consult others? How well are professionals coping with a more fragmented and diverse society. Or is it the case that the voice of young people often gets drowned out by other dominant voices that professionals have to listen to?

Young people need to understand their audience well. They need to know what kind of voice is most likely to have an impact. Many groups of professionals are bombarded with surveys and profiles of local communities and, increasingly, videos, which they have little time to absorb or which they do not relate to their own practice. In becoming more knowledgeable about the codes and expectations of their audiences, young people are in a position to strike a better balance between being considered and being challenging. To some extent, considered arguments and viewpoints are recognised as such because they are received in the language of the listener, and helping young people to play this game with authenticity is not an easy task. Researchers, too, have much to overcome in traditional fieldwork practices if young people's experiences are not to be reconstructed within the language and concerns of adults. What we aim at in the following sections is to mention research that has young people involved as critical participants, who are part of the research process, rather than an object of its enquiry (Alderson, 1995; Nespor, 1998; Hurley and Duxbury, 2000).

Later on, we discuss different types of voice, and possibly the biggest criticism of this assumption is that there is only one kind of voice that is likely to get a reaction. The key issue, as relevant to the use of video as any other method, is knowing when to speak in what particular kind of voice and having the confidence to do so. A youth worker we worked with on one video project described this very well when he said that, more often than not, when faced with an audience of adults, young people would prefer to voice their perspectives by putting on the video and then leaving the room, rather than face the reaction.

Some of the underlying assumptions about voice have led people to argue for the use of particular techniques or completely separate structures and processes when working with young people, and this is where video comes in. Developing approaches that are attractive to young people and involving them actively in the process are seen as particularly important, because of the alienation of young people from many of the other structures that exist because these are targeted at adults. There is a problem, however, with special techniques and separate procedures, and that is the extent to which the perspectives and issues of young people appear as they do because they are framed by what they are asked and how they are asked. This, in turn, can impact on the effect that young people can have on the policy- and decision-making that affects their lives. As Fitzpatrick *et al.* (1998) point out, creating separate structures for responding to the needs of young people can have the effect of marginalising them. They describe clear evidence of a tension between foregrounding young people in urban regeneration and compart-mentalising youth issues.

In a heavily pressured bureaucratic environment, systems that appear to raise the voices of young people can often serve to normalise and disperse alternative views and thereby reinforce adult structures; schools are good examples of such places (Fine and Weiss, 1998; Gitlin, 1998). The numbers of young people directly involved in communicating and reporting to adults in school councils (Ashworth, 1995) and youth forums (Willow, 1997) are relatively small. Though, in each case, the aim is to make these young people representative of the majority and their issues, the evidence is that much

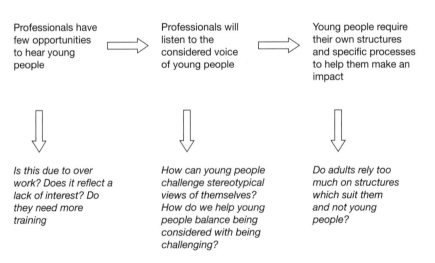

Figure 6.3
Assumption 3

of what young people get to talk about is defined by the prevailing adult agenda. Unless young people are given the space they need to reflect on their own issues, it is always more likely that the agenda will come from elsewhere.

Assumption 4: Young people can get things changed by getting their voices heard

Although there are numerous personal outcomes that young people can achieve through being involved in voicing their views and experiences, this is not generally their prime motivation for doing so. Young people want something to change, something to happen, somebody to take note. They want an impact. They assume, even if many professionals do not, that:

- They can get things changed by getting their voices heard.

But what they are able to impact on is limited by two further assumptions:

- There are only certain issues on which young people need to be consulted.
- Young people are particularly effective at influencing other young people.

For all the effort and time put into the numerous projects that have tried to get the voices of the young heard, and the notable successes of a number of them, the widespread impact of these many initiatives has been called into question. Although professionals have employed innovative methods for reaching and working with excluded and vulnerable young people through youth forums (Matthews and Limb, 1999), there is little evidence to suggest that they have been able to impact on the wider policy concerns of local authorities and service providers. Similarly, an evaluation of school councils has shown them as having a limited impact on practices within schools. As professionals, we need to ask ourselves why this should be so.

What power then has the voice of young people to make things happen? It cannot be the power to redirect resources. Perhaps the answer lies in its perceived authenticity. There is now an expectation within many professions and services that they are inclusive and can show evidence of working with a broad range of groups in terms of 'race', ethnicity, gender, disability, sexuality and age. This drive towards inclusiveness and 'bottom-up' approaches is based on a desire to reach out to the most excluded of young people and is partially responsible for the popularity of techniques such as video. There is, however, a danger that all this activity at the 'bottom' will not result in new or innovative decisions. A failure to change cultures within organisations and services may mean that these voices lack the ability to bring about change, owing to a lack of representation at the point where decisions are made.

The recognition that young people have a particular perspective on a certain issue or experience situations differently can both legitimate their voice and be used to silence it. This kind of silencing can be subtle, as it asks for young people's opinions on certain areas, but disregards their views on areas still seen as the preserve of professionals or adults. The move towards greater representation and participation is still tempered by the boundaries professionals set as to what areas they should be consulted on and the appropriate method for doing so. Students can feasibly have a voice in writing school rules, but not in the appointment of new staff or more far-ranging policy initiatives. Again, the power of their voice is diluted, as it is channelled into 'safe' spaces and managed by more powerful voices.

This final part of this assumption, that young people are particularly effective at influencing other young people, has been partially validated by the success of innovations such as peer education projects in areas where professionals have had limited success with more traditional approaches, for example in areas such as drugs and sex education. With these alternative initiatives, the empathy and understanding that young people are deemed to have with other young people who have similar experiences are considered to be the key to their effectiveness. These approaches have their place, but there is a danger that placing people into crude categories of experience and matching these up with other 'similar' young people can become a very subtle form of silencing in that, if we start to listen to people only as 'homeless' or as a 'drug user', so we come to value only part of their experiences. Second is the question of the extent to which professionals, in building their work around excluded groups and supporting their work with other young people facing similar problems, fragment the voice of young people and sanitise it around a number of 'issues'. For example, becoming homeless is a devastating event in anyone's life, but one that is experienced very differently by young people. Becoming homeless after leaving care, through drug addiction or because one has broken the moral codes of one's community and been expelled are all very different experiences. There is a danger of the pragmatic concerns of professionals, and young people, being foregrounded, to the detriment of the development of a wider and deeper understanding of young people.

These issues became apparent when we worked with the 'Seen but not heard' project. This project is written up as a case study in the following section of this chapter because it is an illustration of the impact of

Young people can get things changed by getting their voices heard	→	There are only certain issues on which young people need to be considered	→	Young people are particularly effective at influencing other young people
⇩		⇩		⇩
What power has this 'voice'? Has the culture changed to allow participation in decision-making?		*Recognising that young people have particular experiences can be used to both legitimate their voice and to silence it*		*There is a danger of the concerns of professionals being emphasised to the detriment of developing a better understanding of young people*

Figure 6.4
Assumption 4

professionals applying categories to young people. They were not a 'natural' group, in that they had come together because they were considered by their teachers to be at risk of exclusion. Most of the group had already been temporarily excluded from school, and some were on the verge of permanent exclusion. The reasons for their exclusion were varied. Some of the group were bullies; others had reacted to being bullied by 'acting out' in the classroom. These experiences were subsumed beneath their common experience of being excluded – an experience shaped by the professionals that worked with them and which gained meaning from a context defined by them. Although there was a common experience of exclusion, it was imposed on them, and given a name, by others, not the young men in the group. As we worked with the group to help them voice their experience of exclusion, many of the problems we encountered arose because their reasons for being part of this group were so diverse, and this was particularly so when it came to deciding what sort of video they wanted to make and its design, and when it came to showing the film.

Giving voice, being listened to, being heard

Questions about being listened to and being heard in the spaces and places where decisions are made are very much connected to the issue of what sort of voice is being articulated, and what that voice is attempting to achieve. Some years ago, we set out a theoretical framework arguing that there were generally three forms of voice dominating current work (Hadfield and Haw, 2001). These were authoritative, critical and therapeutic.

1   *Authoritative*: This is a representative voice, intended to speak on behalf of a group – 'children say . . .', 'adolescents believe . . .'. It is exercised politically in consultations and through elected bodies such as councils and working parties. Researchers also elicit an authoritative voice: through surveys, where majority opinions are taken to be representative of a larger group; through the use of quotations, either from interviews, which have been coded and thematised or selected from a discourse analysis, or through narratives that 'ring true'.

2   *Critical*: This voice is intended to challenge the status quo. It may be directed towards policies and practices, or towards stereotypical portrayals. It may also mean putting into the public arena perspectives that are rarely, if ever, heard. As already noted, this is the voice that social scientists, concerned with equity and inclusion, work to bring into research practices and knowledge-producing communities.

3   *Therapeutic*: This voice occurs in safe spaces where people are able to discuss painful and/or difficult experiences and are then supported to find ways of dealing with them. Speaking with the therapeutic voice is not simply a matter of personally coping, but also of seeing the social production of seemingly individual problems. The therapeutic voice may be deliberately elicited in qualitative research with vulnerable populations. Ethical guidelines draw attention to situations where the therapeutic voice is likely to be evoked; require researchers to make clear to participants the likelihood of distress; and demand that researchers ensure that no harm comes to research subjects. In the case of children and young people, working with the therapeutic voice always requires specialist training and support.

Since then, others have added to this typology. Bragg (2007) added a fourth:

4   *Consumer*: This voice expresses preferences about lifestyle and culture or leisure-related activities and experiences. The consumer voice is also embedded in (delimited) choices about identity/ies and affiliations. The consumer voice of children and young people is much sought after by commercial interests, who do not have the same kinds of ethical safeguard as social scientists. The task of market research is to draw out

the consumer voice, whereas social science researchers are concerned to understand it.

Finally, Arnot and Reay (2007) added a fifth kind of voice:

5   *Pedagogic*: They suggest that children and young people speak with a voice that is literally schooled, that is, it is created by the experiences of being educated within particular kinds of pedagogic, curriculum and assessment regime. They suggest that talk can be focused on classrooms, subjects, identities and/or codes (the tacit and explicit rules that govern ways of being in school). They emphasise that researchers need to differentiate carefully between the kinds of talk on which they focus, and should look past the surface of what children and young people say, to the tacit categories and rules that govern expression.

The first three kinds of voice imply some kind of political change. Through speaking, the person may feel differently, or make new alliances. Those in power are confronted. The person who speaks has exercised some agency and control of circumstances that previously felt beyond reach. However, this is not the case in the fourth kind of voice. In market research, people rarely have the opportunity to have any involvement in how their voice is used or exploited, whereas, with other kinds of voice, this is the very point of speaking up and speaking out. Pedagogic voice, on the other hand, draws attention to the subtexts and norms that underpin and shape differing voices and to the fact that these can indicate degrees of compliance or resistance that need to be listened too as much as what is being explicitly articulated.

Although abstract typologies are necessarily simplistic, this framework is useful because it helps in the identification of the type of voice being articulated and highlights the voices being silenced in any area of activity, both of which are directly linked to the issues concerning the role video may play and to listening and response. The methodological difficulty is in how to honour different voices alongside each other throughout the research process. This is where video has such promise. Its fluidity as a medium means that it can pick up different sorts of voice and place them in dialogue with each other and with a range of images. However, as the research community responds to, and takes advantage of, a media-savvy generation of young people, this creates its own, unique methodological problems. These problems concern the technical and creative aspects of video production, in combination with the relational and change elements that are part of the participatory research process. Each of these potential benefits associated with the use of video brings with it a range of methodological issues, ranging from the ethical to the technical, the intensity of which vary with the form of participatory research involved.

The design of the 'Seen but not heard' project'

We have described this project more fully in the previous chapter to highlight certain key points to do with the role of video in generating participation. For an account of how the project was set up, why we chose to work with this particular group and how different participatory relationships were managed see pages 104–11. In terms of articulating their critical voice through their video, our problem from the beginning was the disparity between the type of film the young men thought they were going to produce and the one we knew it was more likely they would make. It quickly became obvious that we would need to 'pull them back' from two misconceptions. The first was that their film would look like what they saw on television, to the extent that they envisaged it being shown on Channel 4 as a documentary. The second was that they wanted to covertly film their teachers. Technically, they were impatient to start using the cameras and reluctant to listen to instructions about dos and don'ts, such as holding and framing shots, avoiding 'wobble vision' and being circumspect about the amount of footage they took. To ameliorate this and get to know them better, we organised an ice-skating evening, where we gave them carte blanche to film whatever they liked.

We began by identifying and raising the issues surrounding exclusion as seen by the young people themselves. We did this through a series of large and small group discussions, using the contractual arrangements already in place and agreed upon by the young men and the 'Time out' workers. They had already established rules concerning who speaks and for how long, and appropriate language and behaviour.

In the early stages, the issues raised by the group included vandalism, attendance, exclusion, relationships with teachers, being listened to, motivation, behaviour and achievement. Throughout these stages, as the group explored these issues, they were particularly good at taking account of the views of others. The result of this process was a statement that some of them bought into more wholeheartedly than others, part of which said:

> The school system is unfair . . . You skive and you get excluded. Teachers don't listen to you . . . In school you don't get to talk about important things.

This formed the basis for them to make decisions about the content of their own video. To help us do this, we used an innovative, twelve-stage model for producing video materials that promote change, as a means of helping young people articulate their voice (Schouten and Watling, 1997).

Together with the 'Time out' workers, we encouraged these young men to take on the responsibility of organising themselves and making their own decisions. They were adamant, from the outset, that they wanted to make a video about the unfairness of the school system, the ways in which they had been singled out for attention and the ways in which they were frequently denied any real say in their treatment. In getting these points across, the young men decided to do a mixture of vox pop interviews in the area, asking people on the street what they thought about young people, their behaviour and who was responsible for it, and more formal interviews with their teachers and other multi-agency professionals. Early on in the project, we asked them to nominate a 'safe' teacher to work with them as well. There were several reasons for us doing this. First, by knowing what was happening in the project, the teacher was able to give reassurance about the work to other members of staff, particularly those who already had misgivings, seeing the work as a reward for bad behaviour. Second, to give them advice as to what would be acceptable and appropriate content, given that they wanted to show the film in school, and, while putting across their voice, it was important that they did not alienate their audience.

As they organised and filmed these interviews and reviewed the resultant footage, it became evident that many in the group viewed this as work, and 'boring' work at that. Although they were happy endlessly to watch the footage from their ice-skating and other social events in which they were the star performers, they were more than reluctant to log video they had shot and make editing decisions about what bits they wanted to discard. At this point, enthusiasm dwindled, and we had to rely on one or two members of the group.

To rekindle interest, and through the influence of the 'safe' teacher, who was a drama teacher, we put the idea of doing a drama to them. They were happy with this and decided that they wanted to recreate an exclusion panel featuring local education officials, a head teacher, governors, other relevant teachers and parents. In this drama, they took the role of the adults, and the research team became them. There was no script, but they took three issues from their original statement to shape the debate. To begin their reconstruction, they set up a formal interview panel arrangement and introduced themselves by name and role.

Through our own work with young people, and as we have engaged in discussion with others working in a similar way, we have noted an increase in the use of dramaturgical approaches. We think there are several reasons for this. First, it allows people to 'hide in plain view', because it can be both a representation and a non-representation at the same time. By giving a degree of anonymity to something that is innately not anonymous and fictionally presenting real issues, often on sensitive subjects, it mitigates some of the ethical issue faced by researchers working with video and voice, and particularly the voices of young people. Second, it both appeals to young people and structures their work. It allows for a way of working with the voices of young people that can be both considered and, in the process of developing the drama, emotional and not purely rational. Third, as the young men working on the 'Seen but not heard' project found, watching a series of interviews can be quite boring, and so it is a way of engaging young people in debates that is entertaining, without going down the route of the 'worthy' documentary.

Storyboarding the final edit was another hurdle. Again, to keep momentum, we decided that a change of environment would help. In this stage we worked at the university. The final video product adopted a newsreel format, with university students taking the parts of newsreaders, introducing what the film was about as a news item and starting each section of the film by reading out parts of the statement.

The group was quite specific about the audience that they wanted to reach. They made it clear that this was a problem that needed to be addressed by professionals involved in education. They turned down any suggestion that it might be a good idea to show it to their families or to the community at large. A preview copy of the final video was passed on to the acting head of the school, who viewed it together with the new head teacher and a member of the governing body. They expressed serious reservations about the tape, saying that it was undoubtedly powerful and impressive, but too one-sided and emotive, as the following quote from a letter makes clear:

> I don't think that it's going to fit in with the approach we need at the moment. We are giving staff unconditional support, challenging them with something as contentious as this is not what we need at the moment . . . There's a culture out there that we can't allow into the school, you may be able to get involved in challenging that culture.
>
> (Acting head teacher)

The school had a particular concern that the film used the real name of the school and individuals in the dramatic reconstruction of an exclusion panel; they were evidently fearful of the effect that showing the film might have, at a time when the school had failed its inspections and was about to go into special measures. Although the head teacher told us that he was committed to listen to, and recognise, the point of view of these young people and felt this was not only important but also part of the solution to the school's problems, that commitment was outweighed by the fact that he felt the video was too powerful and would have the effect of demoralising further an already demoralised staff.

As part of our confidentiality agreement, we had negotiated with the school that they would preview the completed video. They proposed several extensive and time-consuming changes to the tape. As researchers, we were very concerned about these changes, because they would have shaped the way in which the voice of the young men would have been heard. Particularly problematic was the requirement to include a description of the young people as atypical of the school population, because of their low levels of literacy and because they were 'behaviourally challenging'. Considering the vastly different power positions held by the pupils and the managers of the school, and the fact that the video was only to be shown within the school context where these pupils were already, we felt this to be a somewhat cynical attempt at undermining these young people's voice and that we would be guilty of clearly positioning it as less authentic if we agreed. In the end, the young people decided not to make the requested changes. As a result, the video could not be shown to its intended audience within the school. The reaction of the young men was one of anger and frustration and a feeling of having been discounted yet again. The 'Time out' workers were very much in sympathy and agreement with the young people. After some discussion, a limited viewing, involving those at the school who had already seen the video, together with the young men, was finally agreed.

Those that did view the video (the newly appointed head teacher, the chair of governors and the acting head teacher) were among the most influential people within the school. Few incoming head teachers would have had the benefit of hearing the views of their most marginalised pupils presented in such a structured and powerful way. Those managers that had already seen the video restricted its further dissemination and the lessons it contained about working with these young people. The school was eventually closed because of its poor performance, and, in retrospect, the new head teacher had in part been appointed to do this quietly and smoothly. The video had indirectly highlighted extremely unprofessional conduct by staff; the pupils had tended to treat this as 'normal', and it indicated a failure to educate these pupils. The reasons in the letter from the head teacher describing a culture 'outside' the school, in the local community, that could not be allowed into the school was a somewhat cynical attempt to direct attention away from an internal organisational culture that, if it had been disclosed outside, could well have attracted media attention.

To an extent, the project achieved its aim of providing a voice to a group of young people who were at risk of exclusion. The aim of working with pupils whose families have been subject to multi-agency preventive work did not become an explicit part of the project. During the initial group work, the young people did raise issues concerning the work of professionals other than teachers, including social workers, police and educational welfare workers, and they did attempt to involve the educational welfare service in their project. Unfortunately, an avenue for gaining a wider perspective was closed off to these young people when, despite much effort on their part, they were let down twice by educational welfare officers who failed to arrive for interviews. In general, the views expressed by the young people concerning multi-agency groups working within the community and those more closely associated with their school remained largely anecdotal and unexamined, but their dramatic reconstruction of an exclusion panel did provide some insights into how they view and construct the influential and powerful adults who worked with them.

The project itself, and the issues it provoked, seems to us to be marked by several tensions. Some of these can be located within and between the three main organisations involved in the design of the project: the school, the 'Time out' project and the researchers:

- At the outset, the researchers had different expectations and ambitions for the project, different perspectives on the notion of voice and different ideas about the value of video in prompting change.
- The 'Time out' project workers wanted to establish good working relationships with the school, but also to maintain the trust of the young men, who saw them as 'different'.
- The school viewed the project as an intervention for 'difficult' youngsters, in the sense that it provided them with some educational benefit, but never expected it to challenge their policies on exclusion.
- The group wanted to create a new identity for themselves at the project, but also felt they had a role in the school, to which they remained loyal and still felt a strong attachment.

In the course of the project, we were able to provide an opportunity for a group of excluded young people to consider what they want to say to some of the influential adults who affected their lives, and then to prepare this in a powerful and unusual way. In terms of our initial research aims, the project had been a success. We had also created an intrinsically worthwhile process for the young men. Although angered by the reaction of the school, this strengthened their understanding of their experiences and provided a very different insight into the micro-politics of their school to the one of being excluded. Overall, however, this project, more than any others we have done, highlighted the tensions between the video production process, the group dynamics and articulation of voice.

What is the potential of video to articulate voice?

The video, as both a technical and a creative process, shaped our own thinking and placed additional demands on how we managed our work with the group. The research team all kept research journals during the project, and, to begin this section, we want to use the journal entry of one team member, who was a novice researcher when it came to working with video.

> Matching what these young people were 'saying' and what they brought with them, to what we were implicitly demanding of them is an ongoing process that we should have managed better than we did. We were not reflective enough about our own processes and demands ... too instrumental in applying a video production process to our research and thinking.
>
> (Journal entry, 18/6/1998)

At the beginning of the research, introducing the video-based process and the technical aspects of video production could easily dominate discussions with the group.

> Why use video? This for me is an important question in that we have them speaking to each other, them asking people questions, lots of talking but no 'voice'. So what then is the advantage of using video that is different in this context from using other research tools? What should video be able to do and have we really talked to the group about this. What are we going to come out with, one video, two videos, who are

we going to show them to and how? I just have the feeling at the moment that the technology has closed down rather than opened up what I think the model is all about.

(Journal entry, 21/3/1998)

There was also the lag between introducing the video and the group feeling comfortable with it, which limited its ability to prompt self-reflection.

We have not been able so far to develop their 'voice' in terms of self-research/self-reflection. I am sure that using video should help us to do this but we haven't been able to do so to date.

(Journal entry, 21/3/1998)

Possibly the most problematic issue was that the 'natural' rhythm of demands that video production placed on the group did not match with the development of our relationship with them and their own internal dynamic as a group.

They say, 'We are swearing, smoking, go-carting, skating, eating free stuff, getting more free stuff out of people, doing and seeing new things, playing with equipment, talking when we feel like it, making people listen to us, do first think later, just do and see what happens, getting a reaction for the sake of it and pushing people's buttons once you've found them. If any one of those things gets boring we'll jump to another one.' That's what the young people came to us with. That's what they left us with. We said to them: 'We need order, processes, listening, thinking, reflecting, long-term stuff, overview and democratic decision-making. We'll help you to give us this stuff, but it's up to you, because this is yours and it's about you.' Some of our demands connected with those at school and others had little connection with their lives at all. The last, democratic decision-making was very useful in getting the job done, but from Gary's point of view it was 'Take it or leave it'.

(Journal entry, 17/6/1998)

As the production of the video progressed, it became more and more obvious to us that the process had real potential, but there were also several drawbacks and constraints. Some were about time and resources. We had to produce the video within the framework of a highly structured programme (one session a week, every Wednesday morning). Other issues were more to do with the group and its dynamics. There were members of the group who were highly motivated by the video, so much so that they put in extra time and were willing to keep working with us for longer than we had originally planned, but they found it difficult to bring the rest of the group along, and this led to issues about whose views were being presented. The voice this group wanted to articulate was highly dependent on who they thought would listen. They were happy to show their film to the researchers and the 'Time out' team, as we were all considered to be 'safe'. They initially lacked the confidence to show their work to the school staff, with whom they had poor relationships, and this meant they rarely regarded them as the audience for their work. The final set of issues concerned the video process, which is dependent on a critical voice being linked to critical reflection, which is hard to achieve and sustain; it is a creative process that requires immersion in the work and 'permission' to experiment, and it is a collaborative process to which access needs to be negotiated, so that it is sensitive to differing needs.

Taken together, differing issues led us to create Table 6.1, as we drew together the possibilities and issues associated with using video to help young people articulate their voice and get it heard.

Managing the tension between the research relationship and the critical space of a marginalised group is crucial. Marginalised groups of the kind we have been working with are likely to have been denied the critical space from which to explore their own perspective of the issues that directly affect their lives. Asking them to work in this way is, therefore, more difficult and more important. Practitioners and researchers working with marginalised groups should not assume that they are 'ready' to act critically. It is important to develop and provide critical spaces within the project, and to remember that you are asking them to develop a new kind of critical voice – one that they may be hesitant to use when exploring issues that are closest to them. Researchers are involved in a process that requires them to find a balance between the need to develop relationships with a marginalised group, based on trust and respect, and the need to challenge the perspectives of the group. Marginalised groups frequently maintain perspectives that are self-supporting and that are crucial to maintaining their identity and resistance. One example from this project would be the young men's belief that family and school are *not* both connected to the issue of exclusion. Researchers need to strike a balance between allowing such perspectives to be articulated and encouraging them to be challenged. Researchers and practitioners who work with an unproblematised notion of voice may unwittingly fail to challenge some of these self-supporting perspectives. One way of avoiding this is to use 'insiders', such as the drama teacher in this project, who was able to provide the group with information about the way their voice was likely to be received

Table 6.1 Issues about voice: potential of video and methodological issues

Issues about voice	Methodological potential	Methodological issues
Young people's voice is articulated in a number of forms	Allows for the use of a variety of visual means to articulate different voices	Young people's expectations of video are grounded in everyday notions of the media to produce slick, 'zappy' professional videos that stand alongside those seen on television. Their video consumption, their aesthetic, outstrips their capacity for production.
Voice needs to be supported by critical literacy to put together coherent arguments	Video can play with arguments – it can juxtapose, it can pose arguments in different ways and in a variety of visual and verbal forms	Young people can become constrained by treating video more as a closed programme format that puts forward a specific argument. Supporting researchers need to provide creative and technical input to offset this, but can also be pressurised by the need to make a 'programme' or output. How to balance the need to provide support and training while still maintaining a sense of 'authenticity' of the young people's voice?
Voice is premised on the notion of an audience but is dependent on who can be influenced and who is listening	Video has the potential to be used with a range of audiences at different times and in a range of contexts. It can 'stand alone' or be used in combination with other inputs	Young people's experience of video is mainly expressive rather than persuasive. How then do researchers balance the need to support their desire to present their views with the intention of changing the perceptions and actions of the audience? They can also be under-confident and

Table 6.1 Continued

Issues about voice	Methodological potential	Methodological issues
		unsure that their audiences can be persuaded by the medium and uncomfortable with presenting themselves within their own community.
Voice needs to be linked to a critical awareness based upon individual and collective reflection	The production of a video is generally a collaborative creative and technical process. Within such a process numerous decisions are made about what to include and what to edit out. This can promote critical awareness and reflection	Participation and ownership throughout the process can be extremely difficult to manage. The more chaotic the lives of the young people, the more contentious the issues involved, the more difficult it can be to engage young people critically and reflectively throughout the process.
In most cases there is a cacophony of different voices	Video provides access to a dominant form of mass communication that is also cheap to produce. It can 'pop up' in different places at different times and has the potential therefore to be subversive	Young people can find it very hard to believe they could have an authoritative voice or that what they perceived as ordinary lives could be 'worth' documenting. They are too used to other, more dominant voices, such as those of the professionals they encounter drowning out theirs.

within the school and who was willing to 'introduce' the tape to other staff and ease its passage into the institution.

If you are going to use video to give young people, or any marginalised group, a voice, then you need to recognise that you are not going to be given a period of silence in which to speak. We live in a context where even political leaders use YouTube to get across their points, and you are going to be facing a cacophony of voices, and probably very little dialogue. The key challenge in the nexus between video and voice is to create a space to allow for dialogues to take place. Using traditional structures and systems to do this means you will require some form of entrée, not only to bypass the gatekeepers who control access, but also to avoid being drowned out by the mainstream chatter dominated by formal research, consultations and policy-development activities etc. In contrast, if you try and use alternative systems and structures to get voices heard, you may find no one is listening. The Internet may appear to be an appealing venue for getting the video 'out there', but it is also a great hiding place and digital graveyard. Research that aims to give any group a voice takes you out of the video production process and puts you into the distribution business, and this requires a different set of skills and presents additional ethical challenges.

The case study of the 'Seen but not heard' project identified several critical points or potential deal-breakers we came across when negotiating the focus of their film and facilitating its screening. Our major concerns surrounded issues of managing relationships with the young people, dealing with group dynamics, maintaining involvement and getting young people to recognise the technical, ethical and legal issues associated with video production. There were also concerns around getting others to take the views of these young people seriously and mediating between young people and adults. There were issues of inappropriate disclosures by these young people and dealing with young people acting up owing to the presence of the camera. For us, as adults in a piece of work that was designed to change the views of others, when it came to the design and presentation of their materials the tension came to be about how truly participatory the work was, and whose voice it was, as we were forced to put a 'strong steer' on what the finished film looked like. It also reflects our concerns about the way in which audiences and funders reacted to how young people expressed themselves, highlighting that the issue of balancing young people's desire to express themselves forcefully and in their own language was a potential deal-breaker. This issue was not just due to the naïvety of young people, but also the potential audience's. All too often, projects such as these are disregarded because of the refusal of target audiences to recognise their own biases and assumptions in the way they talk of and construct young people.

This chapter has highlighted some of the issues that occur when the interest of the researcher in video butts up against their commitment to voice. Video is often adopted for what might be called external, rather than internal, methodological reasons. These are reasons to do with its cultural cachet, perceived persuasive power and potential to democratise the research process. Hence, its popularity within participatory, emancipatory and social action forms of research, where it is treated as a medium with the capacity for mass or non-specialist audiences to engage with the processes and outcomes of research. It also highlights that using video for external, rather than internal, methodological reasons is not intrinsically empowering, because the process of making the video has the potential to be, not just disempowering, but abusive.

Chapter 7

Video and your research
Function and forms

Video within research is a process and a product, potentially primary data and a final case study report, technically simple and methodologically complex. You therefore need to be critical about how you use it and what you hope to get from it. By the end of this chapter, you should have identified the specific functions you want video to serve in your research project and the most appropriate form it needs to take to do this effectively. Our starting point is to get you to consider which of the main modalities you want to work within and then to work on how to balance the technical and aesthetic aspects of video with the theoretical and analytical dimensions of your research project.

At the beginning of this book, we introduced the idea of different research 'modalities' in which video serves distinct purposes. These modalities connect research that has used video in similar ways and for similar purposes in very different research traditions. As such, they cross boundaries and operate within the space between specific methods and overarching methodologies. In the previous chapters, we have discussed five modalities, and we've represented these overleaf as separate branches coming from a single trunk, to illustrate how they share similar origins and, at their extremities, will inevitably overlap to a degree (see Figure 7.1).

The first decision you need to make is to choose which overall modality, or modalities, you see yourself operating in when using video. The main point to make here is that your overall research aims may differ from the role you want video to play within the research. For example, you may be an action researcher working collaboratively with others, and the overall project aim is to give certain individuals a voice, which might involve reflective stages, but the video element is basically concerned with capturing the details of a certain interaction, which will then by reviewed by the researcher. So, although the project uses a participative approach, has reflective stages built

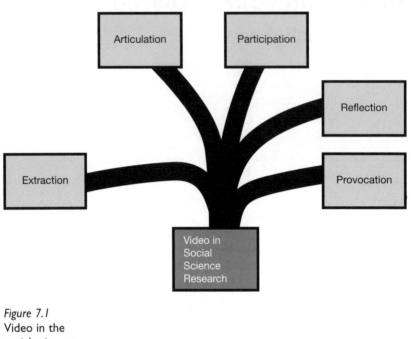

Figure 7.1
Video in the
social sciences

into it and aims to give participants a voice, the video is being used in an extractive mode. The more video is integrated into the research project, the more it will align with its overall aims. This might mean that, in a single project, you are using video in different ways, depending on where it is integrated in the overall research process. This might result in you operating within several modalities, and it is important to be clear about the different outcomes you are tying to achieve with video and the methodological issues you might face as you try and achieve them.

Identifying the modality you are working in

The following task asks you to think through how you are going to use video in your project by completing a number of statements. These statements are based on one-line definitions of each modality. Read through the definitions below; if you are still unclear about a certain mode of working, then you might want to refer back to the relevant chapter.

- Extraction – using video to record a specific interaction so that it can be studied in more depth by the researcher.
- Reflection – using video to support participants to reflect upon their actions, understandings and constructions.
- Provocation – using video to provoke participants to critically examine and challenge existing norms, traditions and power structures.
- Participation – using video to engage participants in a research project in ways that allow them to shape its focus and outcomes.
- Articulation – using video to help participants voice their opinions and communicate these to others.

Now, write down your main research aims in the left-hand column of the grid in Table 7.1. Once you have done this look through the incomplete sentences and try and fill in those that most closely match your intended use of video.

Once you have completed enough sentences so that you feel you have encapsulated your use of video, look back at the definitions and start to categorise your responses and see which modalities are relevant to your research. There are a few notes of caution here. If you seem to be using video in almost every modality, this is not necessarily an issue, if you have clearly integrated it into the research process. If, however, the intentions behind your use of video appear to be nothing more than loose aspirations, you have a problem. You are beginning to treat video as a kind of methodological Swiss Army knife, basically treating it as a multifaceted method that can get you by in an emergency, the emergency being your not having thought clearly enough about your research design, and it has some major gaps.

Once you are clearer about how you intend to use video, you need to consider the main methodological possibilities and issues that will affect its use in each modality. The rest of the chapter is broken into sections that address each modality in turn.

Extraction

The characteristic of those working in an extractive mode is that, first and foremost, they are treating video as form of data to be used by the researcher. Those working in this way are therefore clearly in the territory of video as a means of data generation. The two main methodological issues we discussed in Chapter 2 were whether video was different in status from other forms of data, and if there were any distinct issues that the researcher should be aware

Table 7.1 Aims for your video

State your overall project aims below:	Complete the root sentences below that are relevant to your project. *I will be using video to . . .*
....	record .... so that I can study .... in more depth
....	support .... to reflect upon ....
....	help .... voice their views on .... to ....
....	engage participants in research on .... where they will ....
....	provoke .... to examine critically ....
....	**Summary:** I will be using video in the following modalities: ....

of related to video-making as a data generation process, beyond the obvious technical ones. In this section, we return to these two related issues by asking you to complete two short tasks.

'Laden' data

All data are technically, theoretically and culturally laden, in that these three influences shape our views of the data's status in relation to other forms of data and how the collection process has affected its validity and reliability. To ease you into thinking critically about your use of video as data, we have set out three questions about each area of influence for you to interrogate how you intend to use video. After thinking through these separately, consider one last question. Do these influences combine to make your use of video particularly problematic?

What aspects of your research topic are actually visible?
What aspects of it can and cannot be recorded on video?
Will the video reveal aspects of the topic that participants would not be able to observe, if so how does this affect your other data activities and analysis?

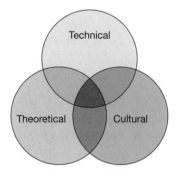

How closely have you mapped your theoretical understanding of the focus to your shooting schedule and camera set-up?
How have you determined when, where and between whom the key interactions take place, and begin and end?
What degree of granularity are you trying to achieve, and how many layers of video data are you seeking?

What cultural norms in your research community affect the way that video is treated as data?
To what extent does your use of video challenge or reinforce these norms?
What degree of ethical sensitivity is there within your research community towards video data and how will you reassure them you have considered these issues carefully?

Figure 7.2
Laden data

Primary, secondary or composite?

As we discused in Chapter 2, one of the potentially confusing issues surrounding video data is that they can operate at different levels of granularity, so
that video can capture a broad sweep of interactions over several days and
contexts, and it can capture minute facial movements within a single
utterance. The ability to layer differing levels of video data is potentially one
of the most powerful analytical tools available to a researcher, as each layer
can add meaning to the next. Problems arise analytically, and in terms of
reporting, when this layering leads to confusion as to whether the video is
being treated as primary or secondary data about the phenomenon being
studied. There is no simple solution to this issue, as there is no agreed line
between what constitutes primary and secondary data. This was why we used
the phrase composite to describe the nature of much video data. We think
it as important, especially for novice reserchers, explicitly to record their
thinking about how they have linked the focus of the research to the video
data they intend to connect. Basically, in doing this, you are setting out how
you have operationalised or problematised the phenomenon, so that it might
be catured on video. Table 7.2 asks you to work through a series of questions
that should help you consider how well you have done this and identify key
gaps and areas of confusion.

Reflection

The use of video to support participants to reflect is one of the widest-ranging
modalities, covering various research formats and disciplines. In this section,
we want you to consider the agenda behind your decision to use video and
the potential benefits you hope it will have for you and your research
participants.

Balancing agendas

In this task, we want you to consider the balance you want to strike in
using video-based stimulated recall, between costs and benefits for you and
those for the participants. Getting this balance right is key to maintaining
the involvement of participants and achieving the insights you need (see
Figure 7.3).

Table 7.2 Video as a primary or secondary data source

	Aspects of the focus to be videoed	What would be actually captured on video?	What other types of data will you be collecting about this aspect?
Which aspects of your research focus can realistically only be captured by video?			
For what aspects of your focus do you see video acting as a primary data source?			
For what aspects of your focus will video act as as the main data source but be supplemented by others?			
For what aspects of the focus will video be a secondary data source supporting other forms of data?			

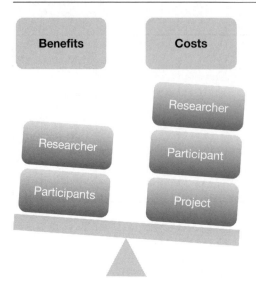

Figure 7.3
A balancing
act

Task

- Step 1: List the benefits you wish to gain in the top left box of Figure 7.4. Now, try and balance this with potential benefits for the participant.
- Step 2: In light of the list of benefits you have produced, consider the following methodological issues in turn and consider what balance you need to strike and the costs that may ensue. (We have given you some examples to get you going.) List the costs of your decisions in the bottom two boxes.

  1 Who decides the focus of the video recordings?
  2 How long and how frequent will the recall sessions be?
  3 How structured will the review sessions be?
  4 What other forms of reflective task might you want to use?
  5 Are there other forms of data you might wish to collect?

Example: a tight focus to the video recording is likely to increase the benefits to the researchers, but decrease those to the participant. A broad focus including areas of interest to both will increase costs to both but enhance the benefits to the participant.

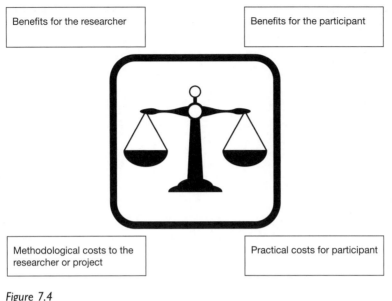

| Benefits for the researcher | | Benefits for the participant |

| Methodological costs to the researcher or project | | Practical costs for participant |

Figure 7.4
Costs and benefits

What type of reflection and what form of trigger?

In the chapter on reflection, we discussed two of our projects by summarising the type of reflection we were trying to engender and then working across a range of methodological issues. In this task, we want you to do the same (see Table 7.3). We have included a number of prompts to help you complete each box.

- *Type of reflection* – you might want to develop your own metaphor for the type of reflection you are trying to engender; there are plenty available, but keep the idea of connection in mind.
- *Roles* – who is creating the video? How will its focus be decided?
- *Integration* – where and when in the research process will the video be used? What other forms of data will be collected?
- *Design and purpose* – who is the audience and how will it be shown to them?
- *Strategies* – how will you deal with the responses to the video at the time, and after the event?
- *Lack of awareness* – why is this an area where you have to support participants to reflect? Is it something to do with the participants, their context or the nature of the focus?

Table 7.3 What type of reflection and what form of trigger?

Type of reflection being supported	Roles of researcher and participants	The integration of video within the research process	Design and purpose of the video trigger	Strategies for processing the participants' reflections	Reasons for participants' lack of reflective awareness

Articulation

In thinking through the use of video in this modality, there are two major methodological issues we want you to consider, which require you to look at your project from very different perspectives. First, we want you to design your project aiming to articulate voice 'backwards', from the perspective of the eventual audience and the impact you want the video to have on them, to the point of considering the group and the issue you want to support them articulate their views on. This process of 'backward mapping' inverts the normal approach to designing these projects by considering issues of distribution and change before those of video production. Second, we want to help you reflect on how you will manage the tensions between developing an appropriate research relationship, the video production process and creating a critical space in which the group you are working with can reflect on the issue and articulate their views. The following tasks therefore ask you to consider your project at two very different levels: the first, looking outwards at how you will get these voices heard, and the second, looking inwards and how to articulate these voices effectively using video.

Backward mapping from audience to issues

This task requires you to work backwards from the ultimate aim of your project to its inception. Figure 7.5 sets out the basic flow of the task, in that you work backwards from the end of the project to the beginning, while bearing in mind the need to consider, at each key stage, the project itself and the role that video will play in it.

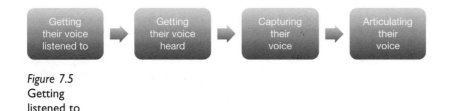

Figure 7.5
Getting
listened to

Table 7.4 Backward mapping your project

Stages in giving voice	Phases in the overall project	Key stages in producing and distributing video
Getting their voice listened to	Who is it that you wish to influence? (Are there multiple audiences?) What type of influence do you want to have? (Does this vary between audiences?) What sort of dialogue or discussion do you need to encourage?	What role will the video(s) play in the dialogue and discussions? Will someone be needed to mediate the use of the video? (Who will do this?)
Getting their voice heard	What type of voice are these audiences most likely to listen to? (Will you need to articulate different types of voice?) Are there specific points in time or specific places that you need to make sure this voice is heard? How will you get these voices listened to in these places?	Will you need to make more than one type of video product? Will you need to have multiple ways of distributing the video? How will you ensure that potential audiences will be made aware of the video?
Capturing their voice	How does this group voice their views? Do they express themselves in a variety of forms? Are some of these forms more relevant than others to the issue being discussed? Do you need to use different means to capture these voices?	What aspects of their voice are best captured on video? Are there specific problems about using video with this group around any aspects of the issue? Might you need to use other formats to capture their voice in these aspects? What other formats might you need to develop to accompany the video?
Articulating their voice	What are the varying degrees of awareness around this issue? How does this group currently discuss the issue that is the focus of the project? Do you need to use different processes to help them reflect on certain aspects? To what extent is there consensus around the issue? How does this influence the group you need to involve? Does the issue define the group or the group define the issue?	How will you use the video production process to make the group aware of the differing ways in which it is viewed? How can the video production process help the group reflect on their own views on the issue? To what extent is the idea of producing the video being used to build the group and to what extent does this affect its membership?

In Table 7.4, we have created a series of questions to help you backward-map your own project. We have two columns: one addresses the project as a whole, while the other focuses on video. We have made a number of assumptions in designing the task: that you have an intended audience in mind, and that you are working with an identifiable group. This may not be the case in your project, but the process can easily be adapted.

Creating a critically reflective space

Research in this modality often means working with marginalised groups around a specific issue. Although some of these groups may have been made highly conscious about the issue by the process of being marginalised, practitioners and researchers working with them should not assume that they are 'ready' to reflect. Many of the individuals we have worked with have been denied the critical space from which to explore their own perspective of the issues that directly affect their lives. Asking them to produce a video on one of these issues may require that you provide such critical spaces within the project. You may be asking them to develop a new kind of voice, or at least to articulate it in an unfamiliar way, and one that they may be hesitant to use when exploring issues that are closest to them.

Constructing a space to help participants think critically about, and articulate their views on, an issue requires the researcher to find a balance between developing a relationship based on trust and respect and the need to challenge the perspectives of the group around an issue on which they are going to make a video. This process is complicated by the fact that marginalised groups frequently maintain perspectives that are self-supporting and that are crucial to maintaining their identity and resistance. Challenging these perspectives will mark the researcher as even more of an 'outsider' and may, therefore, limit their ability to gain the trust of the group.

There are numerous strategies and processes that the researcher can use when working with a group to help them reflect on an issue. However, we are more interested in how you create a space in which these tools could be used. We tend to construct these spaces by consciously manipulating three areas: the issues being voiced; the roles adopted by participants or researchers; and the local context (see Figure 7.6).

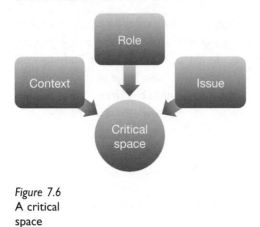

Figure 7.6
A critical
space

What opportunities does the issue itself present?

In some instances, the issue you will be working on may be so specific that it almost completely determines the participants who should be involved and the kind of voice that needs to be heard. A more common situation is that defining and constructing the issue can provide various opportunities to create a critical space. The issue that a group wants to look at can be used through the process, but its use changes as it becomes more defined, as the project progresses.

Early stages: defining the group

Once an area or issue has been defined by an initial group, it provides an opportunity to create a critical space by:

- prompting discussion of who needs to be part of the group; this allows for an exploration of the different perspectives around an issue and the experiences of it that the group see as key;
- giving the group a degree of control over its membership, but justifying the inclusion of those who might not share their initial viewpoint.

Middle stages: bringing in alternative perspectives

In the middle stages of the project, by the time the group has started to produce some video materials around the issue, they can be used to bring in alternative perspectives and challenge the views of the group. This can be done by:

- inviting individuals seen as 'safe' by the group, but who are part of the target audience, to look at video extracts; these individuals represent credible but alternative perspectives and allow the views of the group to be challenged on their own terms;
- showing aspects of the video to others who are also affected by it, from the same marginalised groupings, or who are affected by equivalent issues; this provides the opportunity for the group to be challenged on their own terms.

How can the roles adopted by the researcher or the group create a space?

What effect will the roles you and the participants take on have on shaping a critical space? Although some decisions will have to be made on the basis of the demands certain roles make on individual skill levels, understanding and commitment, these decisions can be consciously developed and managed to develop a critical space.

Early stages: developing the group's understanding of the issue

Much of the discussion of roles within the group and between the researcher and the group comes down to issues of control, rights and responsibilities; there are also the emotional demands this kind of work creates.

- Initial discussions of roles allow for relatively abstract issues, such as power and rights, to be brought into the group and initially applied to the work before being applied to the issue under consideration.
- Discussions of the emotional demands associated with different roles legitimate broader discussions of the emotions associated with the issue itself. This allows for the identification of the most sensitive areas and how these might be broached.

Middle stages: developing critical and ethical relationships

As the group develops its understanding of the project, it becomes important to ensure that the members can engage in the production of the video with critical self-awareness.

- Contracting around roles and responsibilities provides a way into developing the ethical framework that will be used with, and by, the group as the members take part in the video.
- Developing members of the group to take on roles within the video production process can involve them in practising new skills within the group. This can lead to their questioning and interviewing each other and, by doing so, can create more critical and reflective relationships within the group.

What possibilities does the local context offer?

Assessing the potential of the local context involves developing an understanding of the work that has already taken place with the group, the local policy context, the types of structure and procedure already in place and the nature of the audience for the work.

Early stages: developing the group's understanding of the issue

One way of supporting the group to articulate their own understanding of an issue is to use resources from the local context that show how others view it.

- Develop a 'gallery' using extracts from existing policies, leaflets, local newspaper cuttings and, possibly, even videos of local people discussing the issue. The group view this gallery and identify those 'pictures' they most like or dislike, agree or disagree with.

Middle stages: develop the understanding of the group about bringing about change

As the group develops in confidence, it will need to consider how to get its voice heard and listened to in the local structures and processes that it wishes to engage with. The members therefore need to understand more about how these operate, how their work will be received and how best to affect local decision-making.

Table 7.5 Approaches to developing a critical space

Area	Purpose	Activities
Issue	Early stages	
	Middle stages	
	Later stages	
Role	Early stages	
	Middle stages	
	Later stages	
Context	Early stages	
	Middle stages	
	Later stages	

- Build an expert panel of representatives from local groups who have been involved in similar attempts to influence policy and practice. This expert panel will meet with the group members to discuss their experiences and to review the materials they are producing.

Table 7.5 gives you the opportunity to consider how you will use these three areas at different stages of your project to develop a critical reflective space in which your participants can consider the issue they want to deal with.

Participation

Two of the biggest issues within participatory research are the degree to which participants are involved and the nature of this involvement. The first task in this section therefore asks you to position your approach by considering where it fits along a series of three dimensions that together address these two issues. The second task provides you with an opportunity to develop your own overarching metaphors for how you see your own role and the relationship you intend to have with those involved in your participatory project.

Positioning your project

If you are going to use video within a participatory project, then there are three key dimensions that, when taken together, define the scope and type of your project:

- degree of participation;
- integration of video;
- intended outcomes.

The aim of this task is for you to consider how you want to work and the balance you want to strike across all these key dimensions.

The participatory dimension

To place your project along this dimension, you need to specify the role you see the participants taking. A high degree of participation would see participants taking the lead within the research, whereas a low level would see them mainly acing as data sources. The degrees of participation would be dimensionalised as follows:

- participants as lead researchers acting as the main researchers, supported by others whose input is mainly methodological;
- participants as co-researchers who have equality of input to the whole design process;
- participants as active respondents are given partial control over an aspect of the research, while the research team creates its own parallel product;
- participants act as data source.

High

Low

The video dimension

To assess the degree to which video is integrated in your research project, you need to ascertain its usage at different points in the research process. The potential of video and indeed its limitations are, of course, closely linked to different stages of the research process more generally, and these are:

- recruitment/access/entry;
- negotiation of research foci;
- managing relationships with participants and others;
- capturing views and different voices on video;
- design and presentation of materials;
- dissemination and evaluation of the project and its impact.

A high degree of integration would see video being used throughout the process, whereas a low level of integration would only see it being used for one or two aspects.

Intended outcomes

Positioning projects on this dimension is based on the overall aims of the project. If the agenda is based on the researcher gaining a better insight into the group involved, then it is at the 'researcher' end of the dimension. If the main agenda is about helping the participants achieve a particular change they are interested in, or ensuring they gain some form of educational benefit, then the project is more at the 'participant' end of this dimension.

Positioning your participatory video project

On the grid in Figure 7.7, indicate the general area your project will be working in by shading in an area that positions your project across all three dimensions.

Developing a platform for participation

In this task, we want you to reflect on the type of role you see yourself developing in the project and the relationship you want to have with the participants. This is a very adaptable task, and we have used it within a wide range of action research and community consultation projects (Hadfield, 1995). It basically consists of two elements: first, you have to draw an image

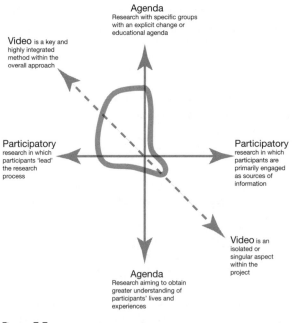

Figure 7.7
Positioning your participatory
video project

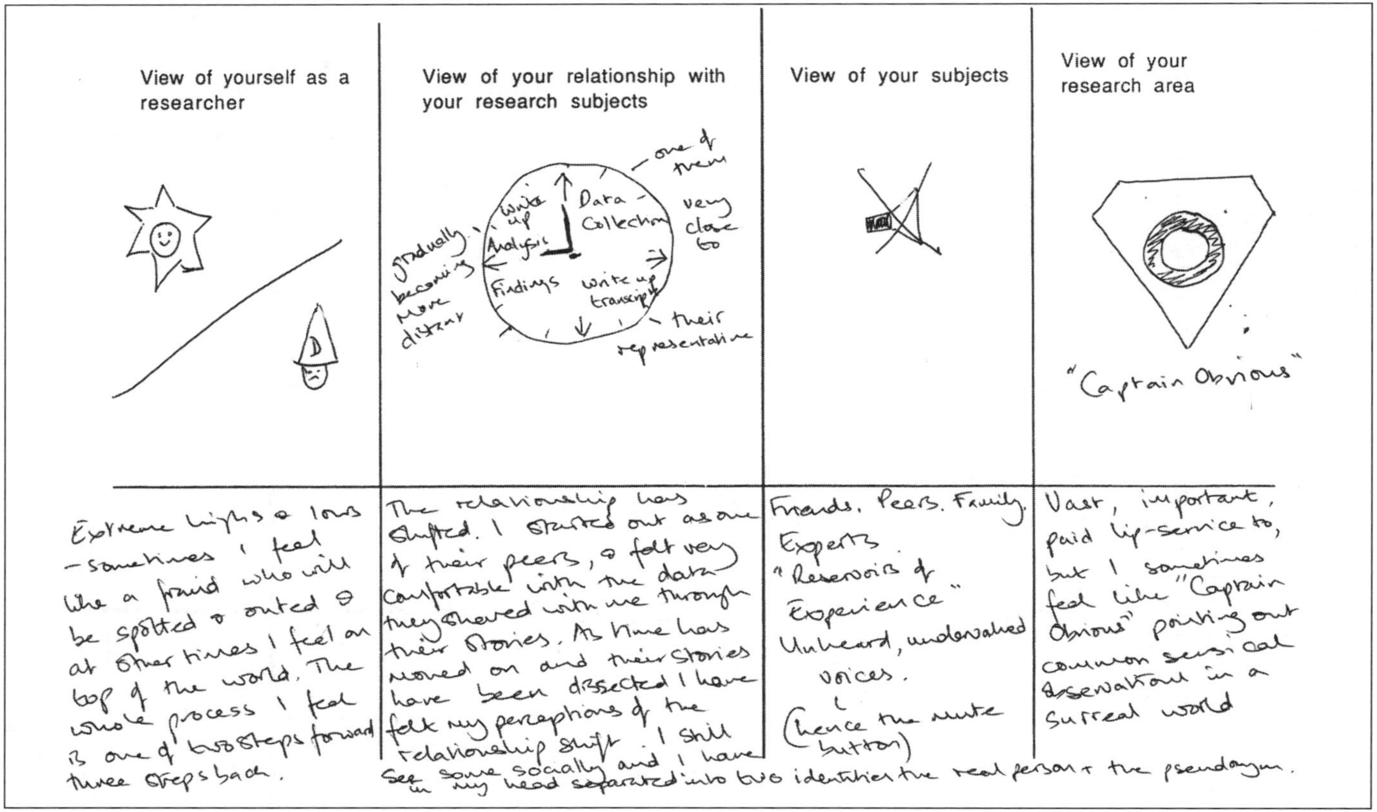

View of yourself as a researcher	View of your relationship with your research subjects	View of your subjects	View of your research area

Figure 7.8 My relationship with participants

of a particular role or relationship and then, once you have done this, and it can be as metaphorical or real as you like, deconstruct the image by writing a short paragraph about it.

These images and metaphors become a platform when you bring together certain ones so that they show the relationship between key aspects. In the case of working on a participatory project with video, there are probably four images that are key to constructing a platform:

- your role as a researcher in the project;
- the relationship between you and the participants;
- the role of the participants;
- the way in which video is being used.

In the example in Figure 7.8, a researcher has drawn an image of their relationship with the research participants using an image of clock face, mapping out the changes this relationship goes through over time. They view their research participants as 'friends, peers, family, experts'; they use the icon of a mute button to indicate that they are 'unheard, undervalued voices'.

These images are sketched onto a single piece of paper, which creates your platform; see Figure 7.9.

We have used this task with participants at the start of a project, to check how they see the project working, and during a project, as a means of

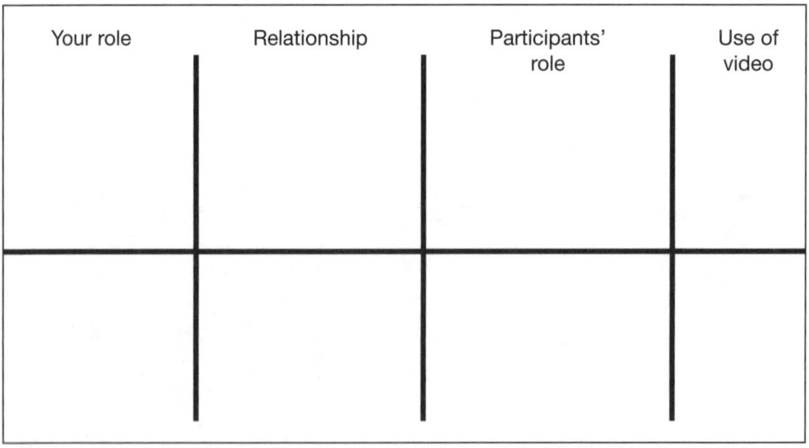

Your role	Relationship	Participants' role	Use of video

Figure 7.9
My platform

evaluating how things are going. This can be done by getting participants to play around with their 'ideal' view of each of these four areas and the 'actual' – what is happening at the time. Discussing differences between the two sets of images provides a means of identifying if things are not working out and how they could be improved.

Projection and provocation

In this modality, the main methodological issues are about constructing a trigger video capable of re-attuning the reflective gaze of its audience. The following task therefore sets out a design decision tree that helps you consider how you might go about building such a trigger tape. The first set of questions, in Figure 7.10, leads you to build the rough structure for the video.

Once you have answered the final level of questions, you can start to produce a rough structure. If you follow our advice, this will be broken down into three- to five-minute sections and be no longer than five sections. It is at this point that you also need to consider more aesthetic issues, such as:

• Do you want to give each section a distinct look and feel?
• To what extent do you want the video to flow between sections?

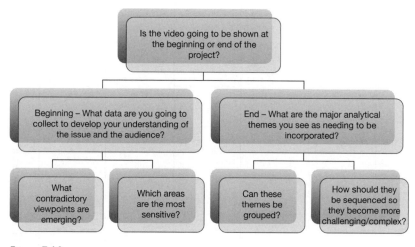

Figure 7.10
Designing a
trigger tape

Section 1

Section 2

Section 3

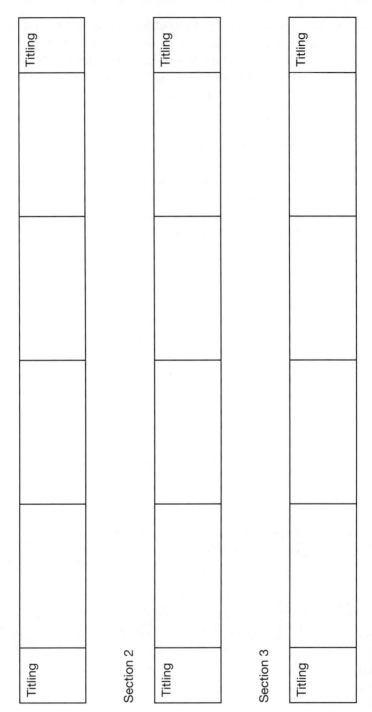

Figure 7.11 Rough structuring

- Do you want to use titling or other effects to focus attention on key parts of each section?
- At the beginning and end of each section, is it worth having questions that can help frame the discussion?

Rough structure

To start to complete the rough structure, you need to consider which two or three key areas you wish to cover in each section. At the beginning of the video, you might want the first section to develop the audience's understanding of the issue that you are interested in. This will mean that you need to pick out quotes and images that define the issue. This might require the collection of additional images and voice-overs. As the sections flow on, the structure of each section will be based more on presenting the contradictory views that either existed among the participants within the research or are likely to resonate with a potential audience. To highlight these differing viewpoints, you might decide to juxtapose quotes and images. These sections need to slowly progress from what might be described as the more obvious positions adopted by individuals, to more subtle and complex sets of viewpoints.

Completing the section within the rough structure relies upon an extensive use of the logging sheets and analyses you have done to date. Once the rough structure has been sketched out on paper (see Figure 7.11 for the template we use), you can add in the time codes from your logging sheets and then start to bring the sequences together. Each section is built separately, and gaps can be left for new material that is yet to be filmed. Once all the sections have been built, they can be edited together so that you can see how the whole video works. At this point, it could be piloted, by being shown to members of potential audiences, and then fine-tuned as a result of their responses.

Chapter 8

Video and your research
From methodology to methods

In the previous chapter, we looked at some of the main methodological issues involved in using video in different modalities. In this chapter, we want to walk you through a basic research design and consider the practical possibilities and problems that you might encounter. We have broken down the research process into four broad stages:

- recruitment, entry and access;
- data generation;
- data analysis;
- reporting and dissemination.

At the end of each section, we provide a basic list of dos and don'ts to help you avoid some of the more obvious pitfalls and dead ends. The possibilities and problems that video could present to you will depend, in part, on whether your overall research design is (a) linear, (b) cyclical or (c) multiphase (see Figure 8.1).

The overall design of your research presents a series of advantages and disadvantages around the integration and use of video. If your research design is linear, then you will have the advantage of being able to consider how you want to use video in detail as soon as you have decided upon your focus, as this is unlikely to change. The disadvantages are that you will not be able to use video collected in earlier phases later on in the process, to increase the level of integration of video as the project progresses. This is not the case with either cyclical or multiphase research. In both instances, you can develop the level of integration as the project develops and utilise video collected in earlier stages or phases. For example, in one multiphase evaluation, we ran several rounds of focus groups and, as we videoed each round, we were able to take extracts from earlier focus groups and incorporate

A Linear

B Cyclical

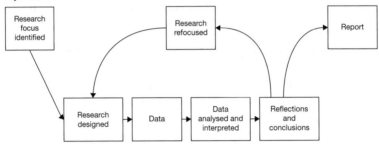

C Multiphase

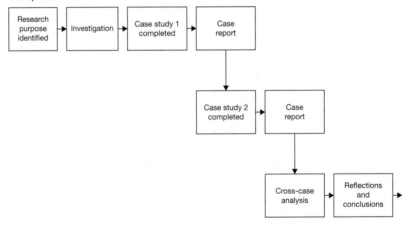

Figure 8.1
Linear, cyclical
and multiphase
research

these as stimuli in the later rounds. We could also use earlier video from these focus groups to help with the recruitment of later groups.

Stage 1: Recruitment, entry and access

In this stage, you will be trying to recruit participants to a project where they might be producing a video, being filmed or being asked to respond to a video. What you need to consider is how using video in these different ways creates any additional issues or presents new possibilities. At this stage, you need to consider the following questions.

1   Producing a video:

- Are you clear about the participants' level of involvement in each stage of the production and distribution process?
- How important is it at this stage to clarify with potential participants the degree of control they will have over the process and the type of video product?
- How will you help potential participants understand the differing types of video they might be involved in creating?
- Can you at this stage set out the potential benefits, and costs, to participants?

2   Being filmed:

- How specific are your filming requirements, or are these open to negotiation?
- What degree of control has the participant over what is to be filmed and who will see it?
- What, if any, aspects of the filming will you make available to the participant?

3   Viewing a video:

- Will this be something the participant can view independently, will they have to come to a specific venue, or can they do this at a venue of their choice, e.g. work or home?
- If they will view it independently, in what formats will the materials be available, and how can they access it?
- What forms of data will you be collecting as they view the video?

- If they have to go to a venue, can you specify where the viewing will take place, and with whom they might be viewing the video?

If you are considering using a piece of video to help in your recruitment, there are a few additional questions you need to consider:

- Can you use materials from previous projects as a basis for a recruitment video?
- Do you need more than one form of video product to recruit a range of participants?
- Do you need to use different strategies for directly advertising the video and then distributing it to potential participants? Do these change if you are trying to recruit a range of participants?
- Do you need to change how you use video to get past potential gatekeepers from how you use it to recruit participants?

Here are few examples of how video could help you with recruitment:

When trying to recruit people to a local community consultation event, we recorded some vox pops to created a short video that we then posted into every tenth house in an area. The video asked individuals to turn up at an event within their locality and was updated so that it could be used to recruit people from different areas. If people could not attend themselves, they were asked to pass on the video to a neighbour, family member or friend who lived in the area. Those who turned up on the night with a video were entered into a prize draw.

To get young people interested in a video-based participation project, we created hundreds of flyers that resembled the types of invitation that are often used to advertise music events and club nights; these directed them to a website where they could watch a short video extract about the project and email the team. These cards were distributed in bars, pubs and shops.

We made a two-minute advert for a project aimed at groups of professionals. We then got this screened on a range of organisations' internal monitors, in reception areas and waiting rooms etc., where people who either worked at these places or were visiting them would be likely to see them.

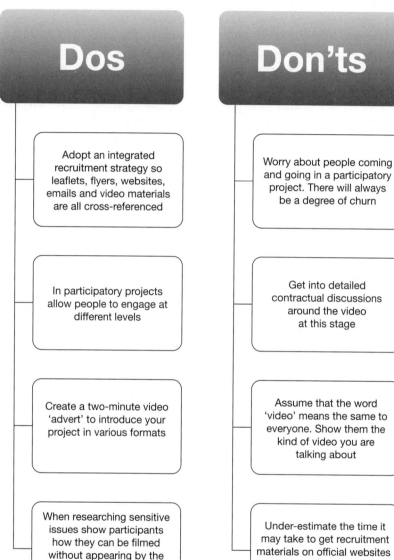

Dos

Adopt an integrated recruitment strategy so leaflets, flyers, websites, emails and video materials are all cross-referenced

In participatory projects allow people to engage at different levels

Create a two-minute video 'advert' to introduce your project in various formats

When researching sensitive issues show participants how they can be filmed without appearing by the use of voice-overs and re-enactments

Don'ts

Worry about people coming and going in a participatory project. There will always be a degree of churn

Get into detailed contractual discussions around the video at this stage

Assume that the word 'video' means the same to everyone. Show them the kind of video you are talking about

Under-estimate the time it may take to get recruitment materials on official websites and approved to be shown within organisations

Stage 2: Data generation

In the previous chapters, we have discussed three main approaches in which video can support data generation. We differentiated between these approaches where the main data source was: *a video product*, the recording of a *process in which a video product was used* to prompt reflection or comment; or the *process of producing a video* itself provided the main data-gathering opportunities. There were also finer-grained distinctions, depending on who created a video product, whether it was made as part of the project or existed beforehand, the nature of the reflective and projective tasks used, and the degree of participants' involvement in the video production process. As we have already discussed, in some projects video may be used in more than one of these ways.

The general questions you need to be asking yourself at this point are:

- Are you clear which use of video is going to be your main form of data generation?
- If you are intending to use more than one, then what is the relative importance given to them, and how best can you sequence them?
- How well have you organised your data reduction and archiving processes, so that you can manage the materials you are collecting?
- How clearly have you linked your theoretical and conceptual framework to your approach to the role video plays in your data generation?
- What are the key ethical issues abut the use, ownership and storage of the video data that you need to include in the consent forms used with participants?

Video product

If a video recording is going to be key to your data collection, then the quality and relevance of the recording are paramount. This presents you with a number of technical and theoretical issues that need to be addressed:

- To what extent are you theoretically clear about who, what and where you need to film before you start, and to what extent do you need to collect some initial data to establish this?
- How clear are you about whether the video is going to be a primary or secondary data source? If it is a secondary source, what other forms of data are you going to collect, and how will these be linked to the video?

- What is the relevant importance of the quality of the sound versus the picture in capturing the data you are after? What implications does this have for the equipment you buy and how you set up your recordings?
- Have you carried out a technical pilot to establish what you can record and what is problematic, and then reviewed your data collection process?

Process in which video is used

In this usage, a video product is shown to a group or an individual to get them to focus on, and react to, the issues of interest to the researcher. The participants' reactions to these trigger tapes are recorded and form the main data source.

- How do you need to sequence and adapt your overall data collection opportunities so that you develop both an understanding of the issues you want to put in the trigger tape and how the audience is likely to react to them?
- How can you design the process in which you intend to use the video so that you can make the best use of the trigger tape? How will this affect the design and content of the trigger tape?
- What are the most effective means of capturing participants' responses at the time of viewing the video? Could these be usefully incorporated into the trigger tape for later use with others?

Process of video production

The process of participants' producing a video provides numerous opportunities for a researcher to capture their views and thoughts around an issue.

- What aspects of the video production process provide the main data collection opportunities? Can you map which aspects may give you insights into specific areas of interest?
- How will you structure the data collection process so that you can gain insights into participants' thinking, both when they are working with you and when they are working on their own?

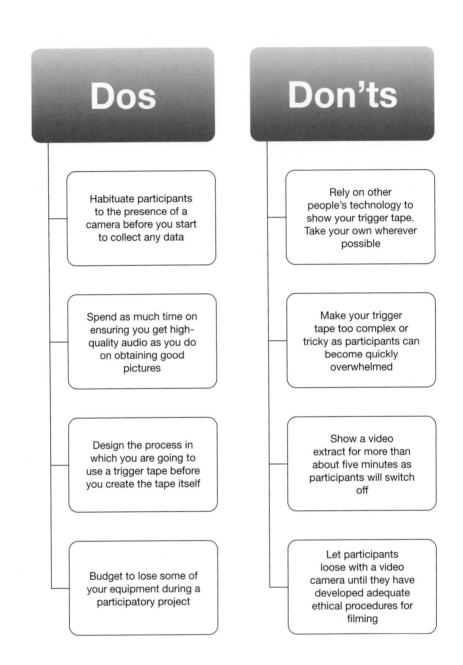

Dos

Habituate participants to the presence of a camera before you start to collect any data

Spend as much time on ensuring you get high-quality audio as you do on obtaining good pictures

Design the process in which you are going to use a trigger tape before you create the tape itself

Budget to lose some of your equipment during a participatory project

Don'ts

Rely on other people's technology to show your trigger tape. Take your own wherever possible

Make your trigger tape too complex or tricky as participants can become quickly overwhelmed

Show a video extract for more than about five minutes as participants will switch off

Let participants loose with a video camera until they have developed adequate ethical procedures for filming

- How could you incorporate the video the participants are making into the data you are collecting throughout the process, so that it adds value to the process?
- What additional data-generation opportunities are provided by showing the participants' video to various audiences?

Stage 3: Data analysis

In this stage, depending on your use of video, you will be involved in analysing the video you have recorded, looking at the materials generated by participants who have been responding to a video, or going through the materials you have collected from participants as they made their own videos. This will generally mean you are working with a range of data, from video and audiotapes to documents and artefacts. In some instances, there will be no direct analysis of video material, for example when its main use has been to prompt reflection; in some cases, it is only one of many data sources, while, in other projects, video will be the main data source. There are two main areas that therefore need to be considered: first, whether there are specific issues involved in analysing *video as 'data'* that are distinct from other analytical processes. Second, how you intend to *integrate video with other forms of data* during analysis.

Video as 'data'

As we discussed earlier, there is a range of potential analytical issues associated with video that mainly derive from its somewhat ambiguous status as data within a project, or the way in which it is handled by researchers during analysis. There are therefore a number of key questions you need to be clear about.

- Analytically, in what areas of your research are you treating video as a primary or secondary data source?
- If you see it as a composite form of data, are you clear about how its status changes at different points of the analysis?
- When treating video as a primary data source, to what extent is your analysis of it based upon the visible aspect of a social interaction or context, or on participants' understandings and beliefs of these inter-actions?

- How have you operationalised the links between the theoretical and analytical constructs you are interested in and the visual or audio record contained on the video?
- Which of these analytical linkages, and in what areas, are indirect and so require you to combine video with additional sources of data?

Integrating video with other forms of data

- How is the logging of video data going to be linked to your analysis of other forms of data?
- Does your approach to logging video allow you to link developing analytical themes in other forms of data to be explored?
- Are you going to use a computer program, such as NVIVO, to help you link differing forms of data?
- Do you want to be able to display the linkages between differing data sources as part of your reporting or dissemination, in which case are you going to develop a form of multimedia case study, or will you be happy to use them separately?

In this stage, the types of activity you will be involved in are:

- logging video records;
- deciding upon the granularity of your analysis;
- embedding differing levels of video one within another;
- moving from the part to the whole of the video record;
- cross-referencing video and audio data;
- constructing video case records.

Individual versus collective video analysis

One of the real potentials of video is that it offers numerous opportunities for collective analysis. Collective analysis can involve researchers working with participants or groups of researchers looking at the same materials. The more structured forms of stimulated recall, where researcher and participant review a video together, can at times become joint analysis sessions, as they both try to understand the scripts and frameworks being applied to the situation captured on film. The collective analysis of video by researchers is more commonly recognised. Working in this way has a number of potential

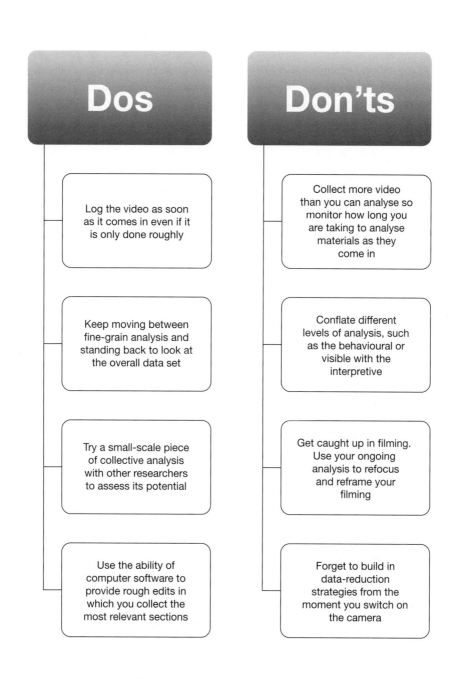

Dos

Log the video as soon as it comes in even if it is only done roughly

Keep moving between fine-grain analysis and standing back to look at the overall data set

Try a small-scale piece of collective analysis with other researchers to assess its potential

Use the ability of computer software to provide rough edits in which you collect the most relevant sections

Don'ts

Collect more video than you can analyse so monitor how long you are taking to analyse materials as they come in

Conflate different levels of analysis, such as the behavioural or visible with the interpretive

Get caught up in filming. Use your ongoing analysis to refocus and reframe your filming

Forget to build in data-reduction strategies from the moment you switch on the camera benefits, from technical improvements to the specificity of the constructs being used, and from how they are operationalised to more psychological gains in terms of motivation and creativity. Researchers have used collective analysis to improve the 'objectivity' of video analysis (Angelillo *et al.*, 2007; Roth, 2007) and to improve the reading across of multiple instances (Ash, 2007). If you are considering analysing video collectively with other groups of researchers, then you need to consider the following practical issues:

- Do you intend to go through more than one joint analysis session? If so, is it important that the same people attend every session?
- Is the emphasis on improving the technical application of your existing constructs or getting in new ideas and perspectives?
- Do you need to sequence sessions so that their foci change?
- With lengthy video extracts, can you get the other researchers to preview them and then bring those extracts of most interest to the session?
- Should you consider videoing these sessions?

Stage 4: Reporting and dissemination

Reporting using video involves differing types of technical challenge, from how to incorporate it into reports to how to present it effectively to different audiences. Alongside these technical challenges, there are also a number of issues connected with how different audiences react to video materials that need to be considered. Video also has the potential to aid the wider dissemination of research and support the transfer of new knowledge and practices, but this needs to be thought through, beyond simply 'making a video'.

Technical challenges

There are two main types of technical challenge. First, actually placing the video data into a report or linking video data with key findings. Second, being able to show these video elements when presenting findings in a range of contexts. These two sets of issues are linked. The 'easiest' solution is to either edit a series of video extracts and then insert these into a piece of presentation software, such as PowerPoint, or to use a proprietary piece of video analysis software that allows you to display the linkages between differing forms of data format and key findings. This 'easy' solution is also somewhat inflexible, in that, to be fool-proof, it requires you to use your own hardware for any presentation. This is because proprietary software files will not run on other people's hardware unless they too have the same program. Similarly, if you insert video files into commonly available presentation software, then there can be issues about maintaining these links when transferring across to other machines and about whether the video elements will run on other machines. Therefore, the more control you have over the presentation process and space, the less flexible your solution has to be.

In presenting our own research, we often have little control over the presentation space and have to cope with using other people's computers, possibly with or without adequate sound, no Internet connection and perhaps not even a facility to play a DVD or CD-ROM. Our approach to this is to consider how we can build the maximum amount of flexibility into the way in which we insert video into our reports and so increase our ability to present it.

To increase our flexibility we have adopted the following approaches:

- We create video files that are compatible with the two most ubiquitous players, Quicktime and Windows Media Player, and can be placed on a USB along with the rest of the presentation.
- We produce a DVD based on bringing together several aspects of the video.
- We have our video extracts available online; we have used sites such as YouTube, from where they can be downloaded and played.
- We create a dedicated website where the video extracts and the findings can be presented together.
- We create an offline version of the website and either load this onto our machine or arrange so that it can be uploaded from a CD or USB storage device.
- We take with us a bag of AV leads that allow us to connect our own battery-powered speaker to almost any computer or to connect our computer to most amplified sound systems.

Audience reactions

The major consideration when showing video as part of a research report is the way in which the audience will 'read' video. There is the perennial problem, particularly with academic audiences, of their literal take on video. The problem here is that, when using video to illustrate a theoretical construct or major finding, audience members often want to 'see' this construct within the video; if not, they often challenge the validity of the video as data, and this can undermine what is being presented. The key response here is clearly to define the extent to which the video is being treated as primary data and the extent to which it is being used illustratively. If it is being used illustratively, then it is best to link the video to the other forms of data that were used to develop the construct.

The second issue is that of selective attention. What an audience will attend to as they watch a particular video extract is hard to predict. The richness of video as data can become a weakness at this point. It is highly possible that the reactions of an audience may be determined by aspects of the video that are irrelevant or tangential to the points being made. There are two approaches to dealing with the selective attention issue. You can control the amount of detail the video contains, by either keeping the clips short or editing them so that they reinforce a particular point, or there are more high-tech solutions where you can blur or obscure those aspects of the video you do not want people to attend to. The other approach is to direct the audience's attention by structuring their observations in some way. With a researcher or academic audience, we might use an adapted form of observation schedule that indicates the range of data being used, besides the video, and then focuses them on specific sections and aspects.

Dissemination

In many of the research funding applications we have reviewed, some form of video product is often included in the dissemination plan. A variety of rationales are offered for producing a video:

- It will present research findings in a more amenable format for non-specialist audiences.
- It increases the likelihood that a target audience will engage with the research findings.
- It will support the research to impact on policy and practice.
- It can be used in a range of knowledge transfer or professional development activities.

To a lesser or greater extent, these various purposes and aims are all valid reasons for creating a video, but, without careful consideration of how they affect its design, an adequate means of distribution and a way of advertising its existence, they will not be achieved in practice.

Dos

Give yourself more flexibility in how you can present your video materials by creating duplicates in different formats

Link any video materials you give to people directly with a website so that they can draw down additional information and further copies

Focus your audience's attention by using tasks that direct them to the areas of the video that you see as key

Use copyright-free or open-source materials to enliven your own filming. See www.flckr.com/creativecommons

Don'ts

Assume what you see as key in a video presentation will be what everyone else is looking at

Ever assume you will have the right equipment to show your materials at a venue. Take a back-up set of equipment and a range of AV cables

Overestimate how interesting your film is or the audiences' attention spans. Keep it short

Let the audience become passive watchers; actively engage them when viewing the video

The key questions that you need to ask if you are considering creating a video to disseminate your research or transfer knowledge are as follows:

- How clear are you about the overall aim of creating a final video product about your project? Is it primarily about conveying your research findings, influencing policy or trying to change practice?
- Do you want to create a specific product that encapsulates the project or make available a wide range of video resources that others can use as they wish?
- If you want to make a distinct product, what additional video will you need beyond what you have collected/will collect in the course of the project?
- To what extent will the video product be a stand-alone product, or will it be linked to a website or distributed with other materials?
- If you are intending for it to be a stand-alone product, how are you going to design the video so that it is easy to use and self-explanatory?
- If the video is designed to be used within specific training or professional development events, will you provide examples of how to use it?

References

Alderson, P. (1995) *Listening to Children*. Ilford: Barnardo's.

Angelillo, C., Rogoff, B. and Chavay, P. (2007) 'Examining shared endeavors by abstracting video coding schemes with fidelity to cases'. In Goldman, R., Pea, R., Barron, B. and Derry, S. (eds) *Video research in the learning sciences*. Mahwah, NJ: Lawrence Erlbaum Associates.

Arnot, M. and Reay, D. (2007) 'A sociology of pedagogic voice', *Discourse*, 28(3): 311–25.

Ash, D. (2007) 'Using video data to capture discontinuous science meaning in nonschool settings'. In Goldman, R., Pea, R., Barron, B. and Derry, S. (eds) *Video research in the learning sciences*. Mahwah, NJ: Lawrence Erlbaum Associates.

Ashworth, L. (1995) *Children's voices in school matters*. London: ACE.

Ball, S. (1994) 'Some reflections on policy theory: a brief response to Hatcher and Troyna', *Journal of Education Policy*, 9(2): 171–82. Available online at: www.informaworld.com/smpp/title~db=all~content=t713693402~tab=issues list~branches=9 - v9.

Banks, M. (1995) 'Visual research methods', *Social Research Update*, 11(Winter). University of Surrey.

Banks, M. (2001) *Visual methods in social research*. London, Thousand Oaks: Sage.

Banks, M. (2007) *Using visual data in qualitative research*. London: Sage.

Barren, B. (2007) 'Video as a tool to advance understanding of learning and development in peer, family, and other informal learning contexts'. In Goldman, R., Pea, R., Barron, B. and Derry, S. (eds) *Video research in the learning sciences*. Mahwah, NJ: Lawrence Erlbaum Associates.

Bateson, G., Birdwhistell, R., Bronsin, H., Hockett, N. A., McQuown, N. and Fromm-Reichmann, F. (1971) 'The nature history of an interview'. *Collection of manuscripts in cultural anthropology* (Series 15, Nos 95–8). Chicago: University of Chicago Library Microfilm.

Bealer, G. (1999) 'The a priori'. In Greco, J. and Sosa, E. (eds) *The Blackwell guide to epistemology*. Malden, MA: Blackwell.

Beresford, P. and Croft, S. (1993) *Citizen involvement: a practical guide for change*. Basingstoke: Macmillan.

Braden, S. (1999) 'Using video for research and representation: basic human needs and critical pedagogy', *Learning, Media and Technology*, 24(2): 117–29.

Bragg, S. (2007) *Consulting young people: a review of the literature. A report for Creative Partnerships*. London: Arts Council England.

Butterfield, L., Borgen, W., Amundson, N. and Maglio, A. (2005) 'Fifty years of the critical incident technique: 1954–2004 and beyond', *Qualitative Research* 5: 475–97.

Calderhead, J. (1981) 'Stimulated recall: a method for research on teacher thinking', *British Journal of Educational Psychology*, (51): 211–17.

Clark, C. (1988) 'Asking the right questions about teacher preparation: contributions of research on teacher thinking', *Educational Researcher*, 17: 5–12.

Cole, A. and Knowles, G. (1993) 'Shattered images: understanding expectations and realities of field experiences', *Teaching and Teaching Education*, 9(5/6): 457–71.

Collier, M. (2001) 'Approaches to analysis in visual anthropology'. In van Leeuwen, T. and Jewitt, C. (eds) *Handbook of visual analysis*. London: Sage.

Dicks, B., Soyinka, B. and Coffey, A. (2006) 'Multi-modal ethnography', *Qualitative Research*, 6(1): 77–96.

Elbaz, F. (1983) *Teacher thinking: a study of practical knowledge*. London: Coom Helm.

Elliott, J. (1991) *Action research for educational change*. Milton Keynes: Open University Press.

Elliott, J. (2006) 'Educational research as a form of democratic rationality', *Journal of Philosophy of Education*, 40(2): 169–85.

Erickson, F. (1982) 'Audiovisual records as a primary data source', *Sociological Methods and Research*, 11(2): 213–32.

Farrington, D. P. (2000) 'Explaining and preventing crime: the globalisation of knowledge', *Criminology*, 38(2): 1–24.

Farrington, D. and Loeber, R. (eds) (1998) *Serious and violent juvenile offender: risk factors and successful interventions.* Thousand Oaks, London, New Delhi: Sage.

Featherstone, M. (1995) *Undoing culture: globalisation, postmodernism and identity.* London: Sage.

Fine, M. and Weiss, L. (1998) *The unknown city. The lives of poor and working class young adults.* Boston, MA: Beacon Press.

Finn, J. (1994) 'The promise of participatory research', *Journal of Progressive Human Services*, 5(2): 25–42.

Fitzpatrick, S., Hastings, A. and Kintrea, K. (1998) *Including young people in urban regeneration: a lot to learn.* Bristol: Policy Press.

Freire, P. (1978) *Education for critical consciousness.* New York: Seabury Press.

Gauntlett, D. (2007) *Creative explorations: new approaches to identities and audiences.* London: Routledge.

Gitlin, A. D. (1998) 'Educative research, voice, and school change', *Harvard Educational Review*, 60(4): 443–6.

Goldman, S. and McDermott, R. (2007) 'Staying the course with video analysis'. In Goldman, R., Pea, R., Barron, B. and Derry, S. (eds) *Video research in the learning sciences.* Mahwah, NJ: Lawrence Erlbaum Associates.

Goldman-Segall, R. (1998) *Points of viewing children's thinking: a digital ethnographer's journey.* New Jersey: Lawrence Erlbaum Associates.

Green, J., Skukauskaite, A., Dixon, C. and Cordova, R. (2007) 'Epistemological issues in the analysis of video records: interactional ethnography as a logic of inquiry'. In Goldman, R., Pea, R., Barron, B., and Derry, S. (eds) *Video research in the learning sciences.* Mahwah, NJ: Lawrence Erlbaum Associates.

Griffiths, M. and Tann, S. (1992) 'Using reflective practice to link personal and public theories', *Journal of Education for Teaching*, 18(1): 69–84.

Habermas, J. (1972) *Knowledge and human interest.* London: Heinemann.

Hadfield, M. (1995) 'Conceptualising equal opportunities in the primary school'. Unpublished Ph.D. thesis, Nottingham Trent University, UK.

Hadfield, M. and Bennett, S. (1995) 'The action researcher as chameleon', *Educational Action Research*, 3(3): 323–35.

Hadfield, M. and Haw, K. F. (1997a) *Single regeneration budget impact study.* Video Products.

Hadfield, M. and Haw, K. F. (1997b) *Family viewing.* Video product for the European Year Against Racism.

Hadfield, M. and Haw, K. F. (2000a) *The anti-racist manual.* Nottingham: Urban Programmes Research Group.

Hadfield, M. and Haw, K. F. (2000b) *The 'voice' of young people: hearing, listening, responding.* Urban Programmes Research Group, University of Nottingham.

Hadfield, M. and Haw, K. F. (2001) 'Voice', young people and action research', *Education Action Research Journal*, 9(3): 483–97.

Hadfield, M. and Haw, K. F. (2003) 'Examining housing turnover and pupil mobility'. Report to Nottingham City Council.

Hadfield, M. and Jardine, M. (1997) 'Getting to grips with "enabling" youth policies'. In Day, C., Van Veen, D. and Walraven, G. (eds) *Children and youth at risk and urban education.* Leuven: Garant.

Hall, R. (2000) 'Video recording as theory'. In Lesh, D. and Kelley, A. (eds) *Handbook of research design in mathematics and science education.* Mahweh, NJ: Lawrence Erlbaum Associates, pp. 647–64.

Harvey, I., Skinner, M. and Parker, D. (2005) *Being seen, being heard – young people and moving image production.* Leicester: National Youth Agency.

Haw, K. F. (1995) 'Education for Muslim girls in contemporary Britain: social and political dimensions'. Unpublished Ph.D. thesis, University of Nottingham.

Haw, K. F. (1996) 'Exploring the educational experiences of Muslim girls: tales told to tourists – should the white researcher stay at home?', *British Educational Research Journal*, special issue on post-structuralism (Summer).

Haw, K. F. (1998) *Educating Muslim girls: shifting discourses.* Buckingham: Open University Press.

Haw, K. F. (2002) *Voices from behind the veil.* Nottingham: UPRG. Available online at: www.veiledvoices.org.

Haw, K. F. (2006a) 'Risk factors and pathways into and out of crime. Misleading, misinterpreted or mythic?: from "generative" metaphor to professional myth', *Australian and New Zealand Journal of Criminology*, 39(3): 339–53.

Haw, K. F. (2006b) *Urbanfields.* DVD product.

Haw, K. F. (2006c) 'Voice'. In Flanagan, C., Sherrod, L. and Kassimir, R. (eds) *Youth activism: an international encyclopaedia.* Westport, CI, London: Greenwood Press, pp. 671–5.

Haw, K. F. (2009a) '"Why ya hideing": the role of myth and emotions in the lives of young people living in a high crime area'. In Schostak, J. F. and Schostak, J. R. (eds) *Researching violence, democracy and the rights of young people.* London: Routledge.

Haw, K. F. (2009b) 'From hijab to jilbab and the "myth" of British identity: being Muslim in contemporary Britain a half-generation on', *Race, Ethnicity and Education*, 12(3) September: 363–78.

Haw, K. F. (2010a) 'Being, becoming and belonging: young Muslim women in contemporary Britain', *Journal of Intercultural Studies*, 31(4): 371–87.

Haw, K. F. (2010b) 'Risk and resilience: the ordinary and extraordinary everyday lives of young people living in a high crime area', *Youth and Society*, 41(4): 451–74.

Haw, K. F., Watling, R. and Sinanan, M. (1999) 'Seen but not heard' video. Nottingham: UPRG.

Heath, C., Hindmarsh, J. and Luff, P. (2010) *Video in qualitative research: analysing social interaction in everyday life*. Los Angeles, London, New Delhi, Singapore, Washington DC: Sage.

Heron, J. (1985) 'The role of reflection in a co-operative inquiry'. In Boud, D., Keogh, R. and Walker, D. (eds) *Reflection: turning experience into learning*. London: Kogan Page.

Holly, M. L. (1989) 'Reflective writing and the spirit of inquiry', *Cambridge Journal of Education*, 19(1): 71–9.

Howard, S., Hoyer, L., Macgregor, L., Maltman, S., Spencer, A., Skelly, C. and Hardy, F. (2002) 'Peer research: experiences, perceptions, issues'. Paper presented at the Australian Association for Research in Education conference, 2–5 December, University of Queensland. Available online at: www.aare.edu. au/02pap/spe02537.htm.

Hurley, T. and Duxbury, G. (2000) 'Engaging disaffected young people in environmental regeneration: a groundwork activity report'. London: Groundwork.

Iedema, R. (2003) 'Multimodality, resemiotization: extending the analysis of discourse as multi-semiotic practice, *Visual Communication*, 2(1): 29–57.

Johnson, L. L. (2001) *Media, education and change*. New York: Peter Lang.

Jordan, B. and Henderson, A. (1995) 'Interaction analysis: foundations and practice', *The Journal of the Learning Sciences*, 4: 39–103.

Keith, M. (1988) 'Stimulated recall and teachers' thought processes: a critical review of the methodology and an alternative perspective'. Paper presented at the annual meeting of the Mid-South Educational Research Association, Louisville, KY. (ERIC Document Reproduction Service No. ED 303 500).

Kemmis, S. (1985) 'Action research and the politics of reflection'. In Boud, D., Keogh, R. and Walker, D. (eds) *Reflection: turning experience into learning*. London: Kogan Page, pp. 139–63.

Kemmis, S. and McTaggart, R. (2000) 'Participatory action research'. In Denzin, N. K. and Lincoln, Y. S. (eds) *Handbook of qualitative research*, 2nd edition. Thousand Oaks, London, New Delhi: Sage.

Kemshall, H. (2003) *Understanding risk in criminal justice*. Buckingham: Open University Press.

Kincade, S. and Macy, C. (2003) *What works in youth media: case studies from around the world*. Takoma Park, MD: Forum for Youth Investment, International Youth Federation.

Kress, G. and van Leeuwen, T. (2001) *Multi-modal discourse*. London: Arnold.

Kwan, M. and Ding, G. (2008) 'Geo-narrative: extending geographic information systems for narrative analysis in qualitative and mixed-method research', *The Professional Geographer*, 60(4): 443–65.

Lunch, C. and Lunch, N. (2006) *Insights into participatory video: a handbook for the field*. London: Insight.

Lyle, J. (2003) Stimulated recall: a report on its use in naturalistic research, *British Educational Research Journal*, 29(6): 861–78. Available online at: www.informaworld.com/smpp/title~db=all~content=t713406264~tab=issueslist~branches=29 - v29.

MacCannell, D. (1994) 'Cannibal tours'. In Taylor, L. (ed.) *Visualizing theory: selected essays from V.A.R. 1990–1994*. New York, London: Routledge.

McNiff, J. (1988) *Action research: principles and practice*. London: Macmillan.

McRobbie, A. (2000) *Feminism and youth culture*, 2nd edition. Basingstoke: Macmillan.

McTaggart, R. (ed.) (1997) *Participatory action research: international contexts and consequences*. Albany: State University of New York Press.

Margolis, E. (1998) 'Picturing labour: a visual ethnography of the coal mine labour process', *Visual Sociology*, 13(2): 5–37.

Marland, P. (1984) 'Stimulated recall from video: its use in research on the thought processes of classroom participants'. In Zuber-Skerritt, O. (ed.) *Video in higher education*. London: Kogan Page.

Matthews, H. and Limb, M. (1999) 'The right to say: the development of youth councils/forums in the UK', *AREA 30*: 66–78.

Melucci, A. (1989) *Nomads of the present*. Philadelphia: Temple University Press.

Melucci, A. (1996) *The playing self: person and meaning in the planetary society.* Cambridge: Cambridge University Press.

Nespor, J. (1998) 'The meaning of research: kids as subjects and kids as inquirers', *Qualitative Inquiry,* 4(3): 369–88.

Niesyto, H. *et al.* (2001) *Videoculture: video and intercultural communication.* Centre for the Study of Children, Youth and Media. London: University of London (Institute of Education).

Noyes, A. (2004) 'Video diary: a method for exploring learning dispositions', *Cambridge Journal of Education,* 34(2): 193–209.

Noyes, A. (2008) in Thomson, P. (ed.) *Get the picture: visual research with children and young people.* Routledge.

Ollinger, M. and Goel, V. (2010) 'Problem solving'. In Glatzeder, B., Goel, V. and von Müller, A. (eds) *Towards a theory of thinking: building blocks for a conceptual framework.* New York: Springer.

Ornstein, R. (1987) *Multimind.* Boston, MA: Houghton Mifflin.

Palfrey, J. and Gasser, U. (2008) *Born digital: understanding the first generation of digital natives.* New York: Basic Books.

Park, P., Brydon-Miller, M., Hall, B. and Jackson, T. (1993) *Voices of change: participatory research in the United States and Canada.* Toronto: OISE.

Peterson, P. and Clark, C. (1978) 'Teachers' reports of their cognitive processes during teaching', *American Educational Research Journal,* (15): 555–65.

Pinar, W. (1988) 'Autobiography and the architecture of self', *Journal of Curriculum Theory,* 8(1): 7–36.

Pink, S. (2001) *Doing visual ethnography: images, media and representation in research.* London: Sage.

Povey, D. and Kaiza, P. (2005) 'Recorded crimes involving firearms'. In Povey, D. (ed.) *Crime in England and Wales 2003/2004: Supplementary Vol. 1: Homicide and gun crime.* Home Office Statistical Bulletin 02/05. London: Home Office, pp. 27–50. Available online at: www.homeoffice.gov.uk/rds/pdfs05/hosb0205.pdf.

Prosser, J. (1992) 'Personal reflection on the use of photography in an ethnographic case study', *British Educational Research Journal,* 18(4): 397–411.

Prosser, J. (1998) *Image-based research. A sourcebook for qualitative researchers.* London: Falmer Press.

Rogoff, B., Mistry, J., Goncu, A. and Mosier, C. (1993) 'Guided participation in cultural activity by toddlers and caregivers', *Monographs of the Society for Research in Child Development,* 58(236).

Rose, G. (2008) *Visual methodologies: an introduction to the interpretation of visual materials*, 2nd edition. Los Angeles, London, New Delhi, Singapore, Washington DC: Sage.

Roth, W. (2007) 'Epistemic mediation: video data as filters for the objectification of teaching by teachers'. In Goldman, R., Pea, R., Barron, B. and Derry, S. (eds) *Video research in the learning sciences.* Mahwah, NJ: Lawrence Erlbaum Associates.

Rothbart, M., Daffen, S. and Barrett, R. (1971) 'Effects of teachers' expectancy on student–teacher interaction', *Journal of Educational Psychology*, 61(1): 49–54.

Schön, D. (1987) *Educating the reflective practitioner*, San Francisco: Jossey-Bass.

Schouten, D. (2010) *Media action projects*. Available online at: http://utopia. knoware.nl/users/schoutdi/ (accessed 05/12/2010).

Schouten, D. and Watling, R. (1997) *Media action projects: a model for integrating video in project-based education, training and community development.* Nottingham: UPRG.

Shavelson, R. (1976) 'Teachers' decision making'. In Gage, N. (ed.) *The psychology of teaching methods.* Chicago: University of Chicago Press.

Shulman, L. and Elstein, A. (1975) 'Studies of problem solving, judgement and decision making: implications for educational research'. In Kerlinger, F. (ed.) *Review of research in education*, Vol. 3. Sage, pp. 5–42.

Snowden, D. (2010) *Eyes see; ears hear.* Newfoundland, Canada: Memorial University. Available online at: www.fao.org/waicent/faoinfo/sustdev/ cddirect/cdre0038.htm.

Tapper, K. and Boulton, M. (2002) 'Studying aggression in school children: the use of a wireless microphone and micro-video cameras', *Aggressive Behaviours*, 28: 356–65.

Tolman, J. *et al.* (2001) *Youth acts, community impacts: stories of youth engagement with real results.* Community and Youth Development Series, Vol. 7. Takoma Park, MD: Forum for Youth Investment, International Youth Federation.

Van Manen, M. (1995) 'On the epistemology of reflective practice', *Teachers and Teaching: Theory and Practice*, 1(1): 33–50.

Van Manen, M. (1977) 'Linking ways of knowing with ways of being practical', *Curriculum Inquiry*, 6(3): 205–28.

Voithofer, R. (2005) 'Designing new media education research: the materiality of data representation, and dissemination', in *American Educational Research Association*, 34(9): 3–14.

Wagner, J. (2006) 'Visible materials, visualised theory and images of social research', *Visual Studies*, 21(1): 55–69.

Walker, R. (2002) 'Case study, case records and multimedia', *Cambridge Journal of Education*, 32(1): 109–27.

Willow, C. (1997) *Hear! Hear! Promoting children and young people's democratic participation in local government.* London: LGIU.

Winter. R. (1989) *Learning from experience: principles and practice in action-research.* London: Falmer Press.

Witteveen, L. and Lie, R. (2009) 'Embedding filming for social change: learning about HIV/AIDS and rural development professionalism', *International Journal of Educational Development*, 29: 80–90.

Index